The worst day fishing
is better than
the best day working.

The perfect world, fishing and working. Captain Billy Black of Walker's Cay in the Bahamas with a party aboard his fifty-foot Hatteras classic, Duchess.

DEEPSEA
FISHING

Anticipation is a large part of the fisherman's world. Anticipation of the trip, the strike, and hopefully, the fish.

DeepSea FISHING

The Lure of Big Game Fish

WRITTEN BY BRADFORD MATSEN
PHOTOGRAPHY BY ART CARTER
PRODUCED BY McQUISTON & PARTNERS

THUNDER BAY PRESS, SAN DIEGO

"Believe me, my young friend, there is *nothing*—absolutely nothing— half so much worth doing as simply messing about in boats. Simply messing," ... "messing—about— in—boats—" ...

"—about in boats—or *with* boats," ... "In or out of 'em, it doesn't matter. Nothing seems really to matter, that's the charm of it."...

From *The Wind in the Willows*, by Kenneth Grahame

The joys of meals to come of yellowfin tuna, albacore, and dolphin from a day off Panama.

For Laara Estelle, my daughter and teacher

Many friends provided me with hospitality, enthusiasm, and critical expertise during the writing of *Deep Sea Fishing: The Lure of Big Game Fish*, including Krys Holmes, Mark Brinster, Chris and Amy Cornell, David and Linda Cornell, Joe Easley, Grant Fjermedal, Bruce Hart, Holly Hughes, Ed Reading, Colleen Simpson, Bill Spear, Jim Fullilove, Hugh McKellar, and my other supportive colleagues at *National Fisherman* magazine.

I am most grateful, as well, to those who gave so generously of their time in interviews and correspondence, including Billy and Theresa Black, Frank Johnson, Frank Johnson III, Wade Leftwich, Monty Lopez, Henry Mitchell, Seamus McGowan, Paxson Offield III, Bud Phillips, George Reiger, and Nancy Wilder.

And nothing at all would have happened without the publisher Thunder Bay Press and the guidance and support of Don McQuiston and Tom Chapman, along with Joyce Sweet and Robin Witkin, of McQuiston & Partners.

Library of Congress Cataloging-in-Publication Data
Matsen, Bradford, 1944–
    Deep sea fishing: the lure of big game fish/written by Bradford Matsen; photography by Art Carter; produced by McQuiston & Partners.
        p. cm.
    Includes bibliographical references.
    ISBN 0-934429-91-X
    1. Big game fishing—North America. I. Carter, Art. II. Title.
SH462.M23   1991   799.1′6′097—dc20   90-20604 CIP
1 2 3 4 5 6 7 8 9 10

Printed in Japan by Dai Nippon Printing Co., Ltd.

Published by Thunder Bay Press
5880 Oberlin Drive
San Diego, CA 92121

Dawns and sunsets, like this one at the Rybovich boatyard dock in Florida, are no extra charge.

CONTENTS

Trolling and ready for a strike on a bright blue day on the Atlantic.

INTRODUCTION

I have been a fisherman since a fragrant morning in 1952 on a North Carolina pond when my father almost fell out of the boat trying to calm me down while I caught my first fish. I remember that we managed to net the beautiful little bass, and that a joy washed over us, mingling even now in my mind with the scents of the pine forest and the musty wood of the skiff. It turned out, I learned later, that the fish was my father's first as well; he had survived the Depression in Bridgeport, Connecticut, and a brief run at the major leagues with the Yankee farm system, and World War II — without ever going fishing. That 1-pound bass became so much a part of my personal legend that I'm not sure any more what is truth and what is the celebration of the bond formed that day between the three of us — me, my father, and fishing.

Facts and logic, though, have never been the biggest part of fishing for me. I much prefer giving myself over to the unmistakable certainty of the strike and the instinctive fight that sometimes follows. Many of us know that primal moment with a big fish: The rod nods and shudders in your hands, threatening departure, the line smokes off the reel, the fish becomes a fierce and noble adversary, and your mind clears from that jolt of simple purpose and realized expectation. No other experience quite matches the feel of a fish on rod and reel.

With my father, a soldier, I meandered from the milder pleasures of bass and crappie in southern lakes, to the headier thrills of bluefish in boiling schools on Long Island Sound, to languid hours on fishing piers off many shores. My father spent most of his time untangling line for me or my five brothers and sisters. We were thrilled to catch something, but just packing up the cooler with sandwiches and soda for the excursion was wonderful.

After high school, I was drawn to the Pacific—to Alaska—where I discovered the miracles of salmon and steelhead along with the soul-mending vistas of the western coast, the home I never knew I had until I arrived. And then, finally, came my first encounter with the great symphony of big game fishing during a trip back to the Atlantic. It happened on a July day off Cape Hatteras, North Carolina, where the Gulf Stream nicks mainland North America in its summer journey along the continental shelf, revealing itself as a deep blue river within a sea.

I remember the two-hour run at dawn to the grounds, the camaraderie of anticipation that infected the four of us in the lurching confines of the air-conditioned salon as we tried to sleep on the settees, and the sea-smells and vistas that so distinctly separated me from ordinary landsmen as I stood on deck. Even the fumes from the engines, though nauseating at times, were evidence of my entry into a new and extraordinary kingdom; I can no longer smell diesel exhaust without the heady associations of that day. Most of all, I remember being somewhat shocked that we were actually *hunting* fish, rather than just casting hook and line hopefully into the unknown.

A good-size blue marlin rose among our baits early that morning, slashing at a couple of teasers close in before vanishing in the foam of our wake, only to reappear minutes later in a savage attack on the ballyhoo set from our starboard outrigger. I remember that detail because I happened to be watching when the line snapped from the rigger like a pistol shot, punctuating the skipper's call to action. He had been steering with his back to the bow, on full alert, maneuvering to give us every chance to tempt the marlin we had seen, and his reaction to the strike was at once fierce and relaxed, like that of a talented athlete.

The life-force of that marlin traveled like a bolt of lightning through the steel of the hook, through a hundred yards of the 130-pound monofilament line, through the gleaming, hard business of the reel and hand-built rod, and into my arms and back. The memory will never leave those muscles, though the fish was on and off within ten minutes, much to the disappointment of all of us. We didn't see another billfish that day (lots of tuna and dorado), but no matter. I had been transformed, admitted to another chamber of awareness in my evolving mansion of love for the sea. Nothing had prepared me for the sight and feel of a fish like that blue marlin.

Until recently, many years after that day off Hatteras, it had never occurred to me that centuries of freshwater fishing with rod and reel were in the books before somebody figured out that tuna, marlin, and the other big fish could be known that way, too. Somehow, the short time that we have been fishing for the ocean's apex predators with rod and reel implies an urgency to record these years that are still beginnings.

And now, I have the privilege of telling you a little about big game fishing from the perspective of a fairly regular person. I'm far from expert at any part of it, except perhaps at watching how other people approach this astonishing activity that echoes with the ancient chords of the primal hunt. Much of the seduction of big fish can be attributed to our predatory ancestry; some, no doubt, owes to the fact that fishing is a perfect act of faith, a gesture to myth and mystery that otherwise eludes us during the more tedious hours of our days. When we lower bait, hook, and line into the sea, we are engaged in the act of believing, and it is the mere participation in such an act that invigorates our spirits. Quite simply, fishing feels good.

And big game fishing feels especially good, I suppose, because it is all that instinct and believing in the extreme. Few people can be near a billfish or tuna—dead or alive—

and remain unaffected, though the same beauty on a more subtle scale is evidenced everywhere in nature. The sheer size and spectacular unlikeliness of a swordfish or blue marlin or giant tuna, for instance, tends to adjust the notion of *fish* in anyone's mind. These animals are perfectly adapted in dramatic form to the business of three-dimensional motion in the environment that constitutes seven-eighths of the planet's surface: water. They have adapted control surfaces, organs, and methods that are wildly improbable — even gaudy — but perfect for ensuring survival in the upper tiers of the ocean's food web.

Word of the powerful experience of big game fishing spread, literally to the masses, first in America and then through the affluent nations of the world in novels and in the prolific genre of outdoor journalism. Practiced by Ernest Hemingway, Zane Grey, Philip Wylie, George Reiger, and dozens of writers, adventure fiction and accounts of true-life fishing experiences were mainstays for many publishers. Among other gifts, Hemingway and the others gave us the obligation to respect the sea and the big fish, one of the pegs of general awareness on which we now hang the cloak of ecological consciousness. Santiago's noble ordeal with a blue marlin in *The Old Man and the Sea* made for great reading, and its metaphoric implications elevated our sensibilities about our relationships with the creatures we hunt and eat.

During the middle decades of this century, the nation's film-makers discovered big game fishing through literature and personal contacts with Hemingway and others, and these masters of illusion passed along their heightened interest. For awhile, a lot of movies were shot in Baja California or Peru because the actors and film crews wanted to be near the best, essentially undiscovered, billfish grounds in the world. Big game fishing became fashionable; although the men-only fish camp

prevailed, many great fishing spots featured spas, casinos, and high living.

For the most part, the first six decades of big game fishing starred the privileged classes, people who, by wealth or vagrant inclination, were given to bailing out on day-to-day life to roam long distances for sport. Local guides and residents in places like Long Island, New York; Cuttyhunk, Massachusetts; Cape Hatteras, North Carolina; Florida; and California also enjoyed the big fish in their own backyards, since they didn't need big bank accounts to get to them.

In the late 1950s, the arrival of jet airliners and relatively inexpensive travel to remote locales brought big game fishing within the reach of just about everyone in the blooming flower we now call Middle America. And lately, mass-market videotape and broadcast fishing programs have brought a new and highly democratized group of people into big game fishing.

The fishing grounds around North America are prolific, though generally in decline; on the Atlantic, Pacific, Gulf, and Caribbean grounds, resorts pepper the coasts. For a very reasonable thousand dollars or so, you can fly to the Bahamas, Cabo San Lucas, Mazatlán, the Yucatán, Nova Scotia, Cape Hatteras, Key West, Cuba, Belize, Costa Rica, Hawaii, or any of the other dream ports for three or four days of big game angling.

Americans are fascinated by marlin, swordfish, giant tuna, and the other big game fish. Even in the most landbound areas of the United States, for instance, almost everyone has seen a wall-mounted billfish in some unlikely place like the supermarket, because the owner took a vacation in Puerto Rico or some other big fish mecca five years ago. Nearer to the fishing grounds, billfish motifs are found on clothing and in trinkets, jewelry, and business logos. Honeymooners in Mexico who have never fished

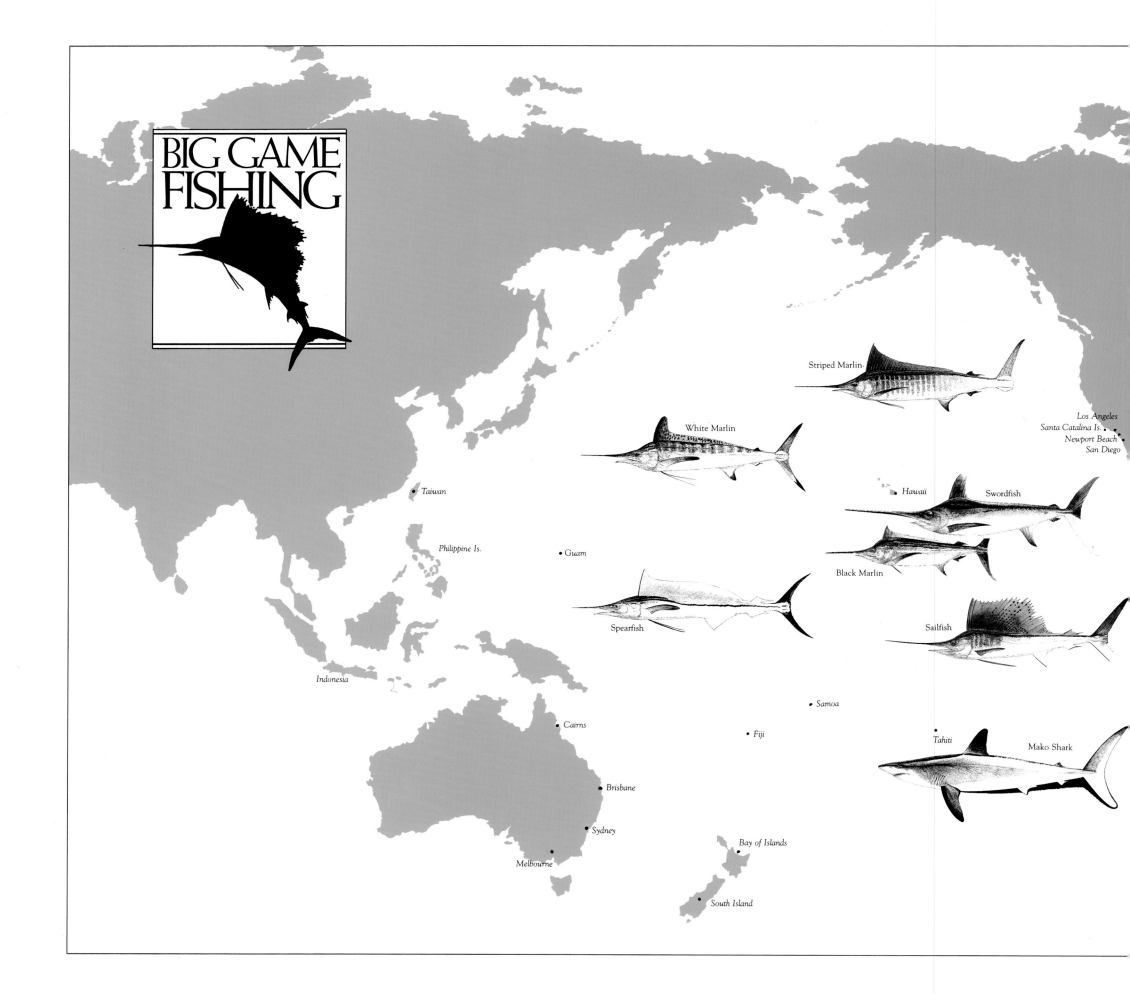

BIG GAME FISHING

Striped Marlin

White Marlin

Swordfish

Black Marlin

Spearfish

Sailfish

Mako Shark

Los Angeles
Santa Catalina Is.
Newport Beach
San Diego

Hawaii

Taiwan

Philippine Is.

Guam

Samoa

Fiji

Tahiti

Indonesia

Cairns

Brisbane

Sydney

Melbourne

Bay of Islands

South Island

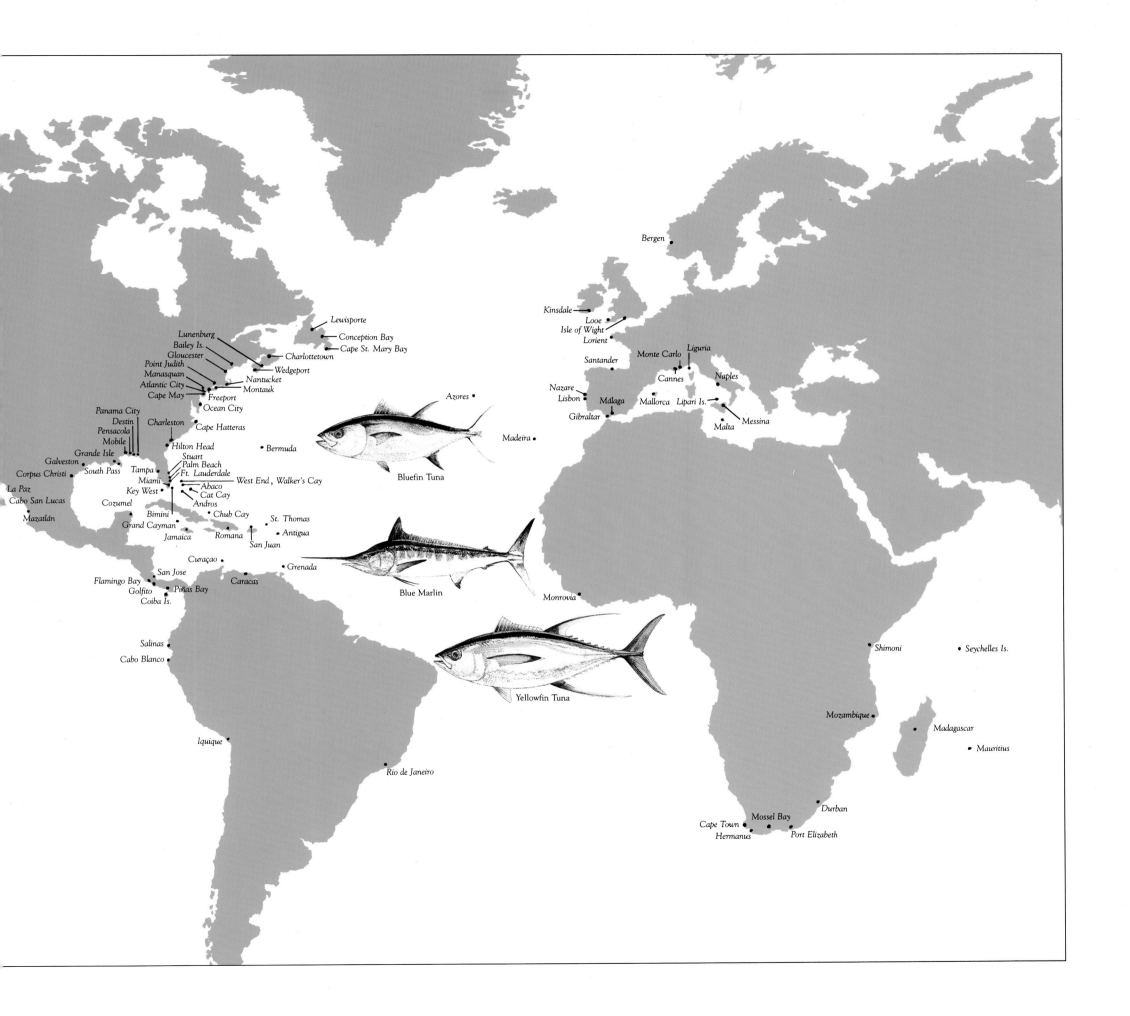

Lewisporte

Lunenburg
Bailey Is.
Gloucester
Point Judith
Manasquan
Atlantic City
Cape May

Conception Bay
Cape St. Mary Bay
Charlottetown
Wedgeport
Nantucket
Montauk
Freeport
Ocean City

Panama City
Destin
Pensacola
Mobile
Grande Isle
Galveston
Corpus Christi
La Paz
Cabo San Lucas
Mazatlán

Charleston
Cape Hatteras
Hilton Head
Stuart
Palm Beach
Ft. Lauderdale
West End, Walker's Cay
Abaco
Cat Cay
Andros

Bermuda

Azores

Madeira

Bluefin Tuna

South Pass
Tampa
Miami
Key West
Cozumel
Bimini
Grand Cayman
Jamaica
Romana
San Juan
Chub Cay
St. Thomas
Antigua
Curaçao
Grenada

San Jose
Flamingo Bay
Golfito
Coiba Is.
Piñas Bay
Caracas

Salinas
Cabo Blanco

Iquique

Rio de Janeiro

Blue Marlin

Yellowfin Tuna

Bergen

Kinsdale
Looe
Isle of Wight
Lorient
Santander
Nazare
Lisbon
Gibraltar
Málaga
Mallorca

Monte Carlo
Cannes
Liguria
Naples
Lipari Is.
Malta
Messina

Monrovia

Shimoni
Seychelles Is.

Mozambique
Madagascar
Mauritius

Durban
Mossel Bay
Cape Town
Hermanus
Port Elizabeth

for anything in their lives consider a day's sailfish charter a highlight of their trip.

The downside of such attraction and access to the fish, however, is that we have created a commercial boom. Offshore fishing is often called an *industry,* a term that sends chills through me and others who are nervous about building an economy on sea creatures that we know so little about, save only that they are part of a fragile system.

In the late 1970s, a profound message on big game fishing was delivered to millions of people in a very unlikely movie, *Oh, God!* George Burns plays the title role as a charming, acid-tongued wit, wearing a white fishing hat with a marlin in midleap emblazoned on a patch on the crown. At a particularly crucial point in the story, Burns tries to convince a produce manager, Jerry Lander (played by John Denver), that he's really who he says he is and that Jerry should carry his message to the world. They play the scene in Jerry's bathroom, where Jerry (in the shower) listens to God (in his marlin hat) say that everything people need to make a paradise is here on earth and it's up to us to take care of the details.

Then George Burns stabs a finger at Jerry and tells him he's disgusted with the way humans are treating the earth, in particular fish. If the fish disappear, say good-bye to everything else.

I don't know whether George Burns ever caught a billfish, but the message in that speech buried in a little bit of entertainment rings louder and clearer to me as time passes. More than anything else—more than sport or food—the big game fish of the oceans and this book are like mine-shaft canaries for the planet. In the early Industrial Revolution, the birds were precious companions in the mines, because they would sing as long as the air was fit to breathe. When the canary stopped singing, the miners would beat it for the surface. So it is with marlin,

swordfish, and the other worldwide pelagic species that are threatened by our abuse and our inability to come up with meaningful international fisheries management. Like the canaries, these wondrous fish can be used to alert our fellow travelers on the planet to the danger.

The populations of swordfish, marlin, sailfish, and tuna have declined in our lifetime. In some cases (most notably, the swordfish of the Atlantic but virtually in every species found off the densely settled coasts), we are in crises of hideous proportions because we may actually be threatening the continued existence of entire breeding strains.

Without a doubt, mismanaged commercial fishing (internationally) and convenient ignorance for the sake of commercial profit account for most of the destruction of the mighty pelagic fish. Habitat destruction through the fouling of ocean currents and inshore rearing areas is another major contributor, as we continue to exhibit little control over human incursion and waste.

In past decades, big game sport fishermen have accounted for a greater share of the destruction, although that has eased in recent years with the trend toward catch-tag-and-release fishing. The pressure of a multibillion-dollar commercial web based on sport angling—boats, gear, resorts—could be devastating were it not for the tradition of conservation that is now bringing not only catch and release, but also better information on the fish.

Catch-and-release fishing implies that we are not out there bringing home food and further suggests that we have decided that we humans are somehow entitled to torture another animal for a few hours and then let it go, all for our own pleasure. The thorny and largely unanswered questions raised in this area of thought are myriad, but in part of this book I attempt to discuss the issues in the context of the commerce of big game fishing. All in all, though, catch and release is a giant step in the direction of responsible sport angling not only because it leaves the fish in the sea, but because the tagging studies are finally giving us the data we need to make sound decisions about our interactions with them.

Fishing people are a natural audience for an appeal for responsible stewardship of the seas, since the traditions of conservation took hold in big game fishing from the very beginning. Within days of becoming the first man to catch a big game fish on rod and reel in 1898, Dr. C. F. Holder founded a club—the Tuna Club—based on conservation of the fish and sporting methods as an alternative to unregulated slaughter: "A year ago, boats left Avalon Bay with from four to ten heavy hand-lines and tunas and yellowtail and sea bass were slaughtered by the ton and thrown away," Dr. Holder said at the first annual meeting of the club. "Today, by your example, not a boatman of Catalina will permit a hand-line in his boat. All use rods and reels and the lines specified by the Club and the result is … the catch is reduced two-thirds and the sport is enhanced. Not only this, but the fame of the Tuna Club has gone around the civilized world, and its example … has been adopted in every land where the phrase 'He fishes like a gentleman' has any significance."

Dr. Holder and his contemporaries such as Theodore Roosevelt and forester Gifford Pinchot began the evolution of public policy with the enlightened understanding that all natural resources are related. Today, when the concepts of ecology and ecosystems are familiar to us, it is hard to imagine a time when we did not realize such an elemental truth. Until the middle of the nineteenth century, however, the earth was perceived—at least by Europeans—as existing strictly to benefit humans and as being virtually inexhaustible in its bounty. Into the waning years of that set of misconceptions, big game fishing was born.

Sportsmen and their organizations, such as the Tuna Club and later the International Game Fish Association, also became advocates and barriers against the previously unbridled commercial fishermen and hunters. Many of these early unregulated commercial predators were doing some real damage, actually extinguishing entire species to bring them to market. And apart from nourishing good sportsmanship, conservation, and gentlemanly behavior, the post-Victorian attitudes of conservation among anglers turned us into potential scientists and data gatherers.

For this reason, the main text of this book is a collection of portraits of people who are the links between humanity, the great fish, and the oceans. I want to pass on to you a sense of life among the big fish from the perspectives of your contemporaries—a modern California fisherman, a man who caught a marlin by accident, a charter skipper, a woman whose life is entwined with swordfish, and many others in the cast of *Deep Sea Fishing: The Lure of Big Game Fish*. And I want to tell you about the fish, about the great miracle of life in astonishing forms.

But after our celebration of the magnificence of marlin and swordfish and the others, after telling you of heroic battles and lives changed in fighting chairs, the fish are still at our mercy.

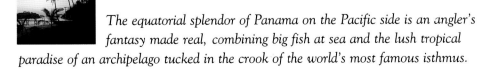

The equatorial splendor of Panama on the Pacific side is an angler's fantasy made real, combining big fish at sea and the lush tropical paradise of an archipelago tucked in the crook of the world's most famous isthmus.

The jungle on the island of Coiba, Panama, gives way to the warm, tranquil ocean that produces some of the best black marlin fishing on earth, with no shortage of blues and sailfish. A fleet of fast deep sea skiffs from Club Pacifico gets anglers offshore in a hurry, and the fishing, especially in the winter, is fabulous. Every once in awhile, a marlin too big to bring into the boat comes along. Local guides who grew up on these grounds know places like Hannibal Bank, a subsea mountain around which upwellings produce dense feed for the big fish.

 Like all big game fishing resorts, Club Pacifico de Panama provides anglers with tackle as part of the bargain, though many aficionados prefer to bring their own. The standards are 80-pound and 130-pound test lines on heavy reels and rods, but recently light tackle has come into greater vogue. Line weights under 20 pounds are not uncommon, and most resorts will furnish the light gear on request. With the drag properly set, a modern reel allows an angler to work a fish with little fear of breaking the monofilament line.

 Among the delights of big game angling is the opportunity to fish for the dozens of other species that inhabit the sea along with the marlin, swordfish, and tuna. In tropical waters, it's worth taking a day away from the offshore grounds to cast for bonefish or permit from the beach; no extra charge for the relaxation. Many veteran anglers pack light spinning or fly rods with them on sojourns to places like Panama to take advantage of the sea's re-markable variety.

A 341-pound black marlin taken on medium-weight sport tackle off Panama.

LOOKING FOR DR. HOLDER

The fishing rod, according to highly disputable accounts, made its appearance about five thousand years ago when someone—man or woman—fastened a tendril of some kind to a sapling. A primitive hook finished off the rig, and probably provided a meal. The reel didn't make its appearance until the fifteenth century or thereabouts, described by Izaak Walton as a "wheele, to be observed better by seeing one than by a large demonstration of words."

But it wasn't until June 1, 1898, that a lawyer from Pasadena, California, landed the first big game fish on rod and reel, and I found the impulse to sort through that event—in truth and in legend—compelling. The man was Charles Frederick Holder; the fish was a 183-pound tuna; the place was the Pacific Ocean off Santa Catalina Island, California.

I found a picture of Dr. Holder with his monumental tuna, along with a credible account of the event. "In the closing years of the 19th Century, he heard of the wonderful game fish to be found in the waters surrounding Santa Catalina Island," wrote Arthur Macrate, Jr., in his *History of the Tuna Club*. "He heard particularly of the blue-fin tuna or, as it was then called, the 'leaping tuna.' He went to Catalina to check on the stories he had heard. What he saw is best related in the words of (Tuna Club) Historian Thomas McD. Potter ∴:

"'What he found horrified and amazed him. He encountered fishing sport such as had never been dreamed of. He also saw with his own eyes that men were accustomed to taking these fish on heavy hand lines—almost rope—and calling it "sport." Promptly, he made up his mind to remedy the situation. Based on his experience with salmon, he worked out a tackle that he thought would be sufficiently strong to cope with the mighty fish of these waters and at the same time give the quarry an even break.'"

Holder wasted no time in founding a club based on sport, comradeship, and the newly emerging idealism of conservation. It was an era when humanity was being startled by Darwin, Freud, and others who suggested that all was not as it seemed, that the earth and the human presence on it was not governed by certainty and privilege.

Barely a month after landing the world's first big game fish on rod and reel, Holder brought five of his pals together to form the Tuna Club. They met on Catalina and agreed to a common purpose: "The object of this Club is the protection of the game fishes of the State of California ... and to discourage hand-line fishing, as being unsportsmanlike and against the public interest; that the purposes for which it is formed are to encourage the use of rod and reel fishing and to permit social intercourse among the members of the Club, also to aid in securing the protection of the game fishes and elevate the sport to the highest standard ..."

The six founders of the Tuna Club wrote to their angling friends, and by the end of the summer of 1898, big game fishing with rods and reels to the beat of conservation was alive in the world. The club's sensibilities are part of hundreds of fishing institutions on which the stewardship of the oceans depends today. The entire business of record keeping, so much a part of the angler's quest and the scientist's need, grew from the Tuna Club's system of awarding "Buttons" for record fish and others of note. A Button, really an elegant little badge, was awarded for catching a big game fish under the club's strict rules. The club still maintains records for its three main tackle groups — Heavy, Light, and Three-Six (another kind of light tackle) — but out of the concept of big game classes

have come the many divisions of the renowned International Game Fish Association (IGFA).

I couldn't resist a journey to Catalina. I wanted a look at the Tuna Club, and I wanted to know what had become of Dr. Holder's dreams of sport and conservation.

Drawn by the balmy climate, the island life, and of course, the fishing, tourists and adventurers have embraced Catalina in droves since about the time that Dr. Holder was doing his best for the fish. I join the stream of those charmed by the place on a sunny February afternoon, leaving behind the millions bound to the mainland and fetching up — for want of a better place to start — in the visitor's information office at the foot of the Avalon town pier.

In the tidy storefront, I stroll between light-box displays of activities organized by the islanders to entertain the tourists. The displays promote scenic bus rides, glass-bottom boats, flying fish, a cruise to see the sea lions, twilight waterfront dining, and a botanical garden. There are maps, brochures, and a pleasant sense of helpfulness, but no mention of the Tuna Club or big game fishing.

Just as I am about to leave, my search takes a fair-weather turn when I meet Betty Quarnstron, or "Betty Q" as she's known on the island where she has lived for the past forty years. Dressed in the orange jacket of the Santa Catalina Island Company, Betty tends the visitor's office as something of a local treasure.

"Oh sure, it's here," she says, going on to describe one of the two big rambling edifices with docks that dominate the crescent-shaped Avalon waterfront. The building closer to town is the Tuna Club; its companion a hundred yards farther on is the Catalina Yacht Club.

Betty Q tells me that the main thing she knows about the Tuna Club lately is that the mayor of Avalon, a woman, has been raising hell because only men can be members. (I would learn that although custom and bylaws had since excluded women members, Dr. Holder and the other founders had specified "gentlemen and ladies.")

"Churchill, Patton, and Laurel or Hardy—I don't remember which one—have been here for the Tuna Club," Betty says, getting a bit deeper into the topic. We talk a little while about how good life has been to her on Catalina and about fishing, in which she seems to have no particular interest although she knows it has been going on around her for a long time.

"You might try to see Packy Offield. He's a Wrigley, you know. They own the island. Packy runs the SCI Co.," Betty says, pronouncing the letters. Now we're talking.

I walk around for awhile, along the narrow streets of the almost deserted town, its charm undiluted without the flocks of people who come on cruises or day boats from Los Angeles and Newport Beach. I end up at the Busy Bee restaurant to ease through the marvelous, flat gray light of what John Steinbeck called "the hour of the pearl." The Busy Bee is a good place for that, with a long bar facing across a dining porch and out onto Avalon Bay, where only a handful of boats are moored on this out-of-season, midweek evening. My only colleagues are, I deduce from eavesdropping, an off-duty glass-bottom-boat skipper, a honeymooning couple, and a fellow best described as a day-drinker who's run aground.

I am most drawn, though, to the 400-pound blue marlin mounted over the end of the bar to my left, somewhat defiled by a candy-cane ring around its bill. Despite its plastic, taxidermic repose and considering the decorative end to which it has been brought, the silver-and-blue animal is a spectacular translation of mere flesh into the perfect ocean creature.

The marlins—four species: black, blue, striped, and white—and their cousins in the suborder Scombroidea—

the tunas, swordfish, and sailfish—are among the most elegant statements of form following function in nature. From the bill, probably a hydrodynamic structure first and a weapon second, the marlin's shape rises steeply into the head and up over what humans call shoulders into the sail or dorsal fin, a control structure that folds into slots in the body during high-speed swimming, much like the wing-like pectoral fins on its side. The principles of such adjustable geometry are also found in modern jet aircraft wings whose slots and flaps used for control at slow speed retract for fast flight.

With my elbows on the bar at the Busy Bee, I am riveted on the evolutionary miracle above me when I pick up the voice of the skipper three stools down: "It's been over fifty years since anybody caught a fish like that around here," he says matter-of-factly, no hint of judgment in his voice. "The owner got that one in Hawaii."

We make small talk for ten minutes or so. I ask him about the glass-bottom-boat business, which he says is boring as hell. I ask him about the Tuna Club, and he says, "It's a bunch of rich guys. They're real private, almost mysterious. I don't know a damn thing about it, really. I've heard that people like presidents have been there, though." As an afterthought, he adds, "Packy Offield's a member. Check it out with him."

Alert, I rearrange my Windbreaker on my lap and enjoy the conversation as it spreads to friendly people on the other side of me. We run the usuals on the weather, the fish, the boats, but mostly I plan my morning. The road to the Tuna Club leads through Packy Offield.

As it turns out, Paxon Offield III is not that hard to find. In a stucco building down the street from the volunteer fire department (whose engines have marlin decals on the doors), the offices of the Santa Catalina Island Company are a modest enclave for a great fortune.

The SCI Co. headquarters is reminiscent of the utilitarian, institutional properties of midcentury railroads and timber companies, with high ceilings and linoleum floors. "Relaxed" barely describes Packy when I first lay eyes on him, prepared as I am for some executive on the run. He is instantly direct and comfortable; and as soon as I walk with him into his office, he becomes even more so, because I see that he is, indeed, a brother fisherman. The room is dominated by a famous painting of a blue marlin hunting; rods and reels occupy the corners. Packy's wife, who stops and says hello, is wearing a silver marlin on her tunic.

Our first meeting lasts just minutes, but long enough for him to say that yes, he's a member of the club, he'll be happy to show me around, and let's meet at Antonio's Pizzeria at seven the next morning. "You'll be surprised," he says. "They have the best breakfast in town." He loans me his copy of the history of the Tuna Club and I leave, the leather volume in my hands—a time machine.

You know much of what I learned that night, reading the history, the story about Dr. Holder and the founding of the club, the rules, the remarkable instinct to conserve. What sitting across fruit and biscuits from Packy Offield did the next morning at Antonio's was give the entire proposition a modern idiom. He earned his first Tuna Club Button and full membership when he landed a 133-pound marlin on 20-pound Dacron line in the fall of 1988. He had, however, caught and released an earlier marlin that would have qualified him.

"My grandfather never caught his Button fish," Packy tells me. "He was an associate member, and I suppose one of the reasons I wanted to be a member. I grew up fishing in northern Michigan but have always had a natural curiosity about the sea. I can put my rods away and just travel around the ocean looking and being happy. That we

stumble across some fish is a bonus."

He tells me that he has lived full-time on Catalina since 1976 and that his life has been lived to a back-beat of conservation. "Most of the island is owned by the Santa Catalina Island Conservancy under a plan originally conceived by my grandfather," he says. "If the Conservancy ever failed for some reason, it would go to the National Park Service.

"I was attracted to the club because of its methods of fishing. They pioneered the rules for the IGFA, and I believed the club would continue to be a pioneer in the sport, in conservation. And I wanted to be a part of it." He pauses in his thought and adds, "Really, conservation is a misnomer. What we're talking about here is restoration."

There can be no question that the tuna and marlin and broadbill swordfish that once dazzled the world's anglers off Southern California have suffered mightily at the hands of humans. Catching too many of them has not been the problem, thanks in a large part to the Tuna Club. Habitat destruction and pollution have ripped the food web out from under the big fish, so they now go elsewhere, as do many big game fishermen.

"The real attraction in marlin fishing is putting together a whole bunch of variables that may or may not lead you to a fish," Packy tells me, describing his own life in Southern California waters. At least half a dozen times during our two hours together, he stresses that he is not a top fisherman, that if I want to write about real experts I should talk to club president Jim Martin or to the renowned Dave Denholm, a club member and a world-girdling angler from Newport Beach.

"You have to monitor the boat, the bait, the weather, the water, yourself," he explains after his disclaimer. "There's no doubt we have it a lot different from the guys who started the club. They used to have a club doctor stationed on the dock to take care of anglers hurt fighting a big fish. They fished from rowboats. I have a twenty-nine-foot Blackfin with two four-fifty-four Crusader engines, and I can turn on a dime and follow a fish at fifteen knots in reverse.

"Are we really competing against our ancestors in the club?" he asks rhetorically. "They had primitive gear but more fish. We have sophisticated gear but fewer fish. A lot is still the same between us, though. My first instinct out there is not to hurt the fish. With Dacron line, longer rods, and the other rules of the club, we took a step in the direction of equalizing the relationship between man and fish."

You should understand that Packy and I were just talking there at Antonio's Pizzeria, that he didn't say things that sounded like speeches intentionally. Speaking from the heart, from a place of ideals, though, brings out a person's best.

"So," he says, placing his napkin beside the breakfast remains, "would you like a look at the clubhouse?"

We walk through the sunny morning, talking fishing, passing shops, restaurants, and hotels of the ordinary world. The clubhouse, I had learned from the history the night before, is the second on the site, the first having burned in 1915. The building is white with green trim, simple and substantial with two stories.

We enter through a side door and are in a room that is little more than a large closet. Known to the members as the Bait Box, it is a cubbyhole of a bar whose walls are hung with informal memorabilia, pictures, calendars, cartoons. Not much of the club is given over to the clichés of fishing, though, to jokes about exaggerating the size of your fish, to the images of unshaven men in a world apart. The real world apart begins in the next room, an entryway.

There, flanking the heavy leaded-glass doors that open to the main street, are cases of silver cups and trophies; overhead, on the walls, are the fish mounted in their fighting shapes—dolphin, marlin, roosterfish, tuna. A stairway to the right leads upstairs to a corridor of Spartan bedrooms. "Just enough to get a few hours' sleep," Packy tells me. Toward the water from the entryway are the main rooms—to the right, the cardroom with chalkboard for landing records, and to the left, the lounge.

There, overseeing several rows of chairs in green leather, is the most astonishing collection of mounted big game fish and fishing memorabilia in the world. The room is big, with windows opening on the dock and twelve-foot ceilings, so the presentation of the fish is well lit and spacious. From left to right, I see absolutely beautiful bigeye tuna, blue marlin, broadbill, bluefin and yellowfin tuna—all representative of the highest achievement in taxidermic artistry. No candy-cane rings here, as I pause beneath the swordfish.

"One of my friends calls the swordfish a soft-skinned freight train," Packy says, interrupting my reverie.

And then, finally, I am standing in front of Dr. Holder, or rather a major portrait of him on the end wall dominating the room. He is seated in formal posture wearing a gray vested suit, his bearded countenance exuding wisdom. Around him on the same wall are smaller photographs of his successors as president of the Tuna Club; beneath him, in casual dress on this February morning, are a couple of fishermen in his debt.

"That's the man," Packy says.

John Rybovich was charmed by fishing as a boy during the 1920s,
and he combined that passion with craftsmanship to found what
has become one of the most respected boatyards in the big fish game. "Why wood?
Speed, sophisticated design, and you're not locked into a mold size," Rybovich says.
"And a lot of guys like the way wood rides."

Rybovich, Merritt, and the other pioneer builders of magnificent sport-fishing yachts set a blistering pace, driven by the wealth and demanding expectations of big game anglers. The most prolific enclave of yacht designers and builders in the country took root on the balmy South Florida coast. Yards in West Palm, Pompano Beach, and Stuart in particular, with seven major builders, have become international legends. Attention to detail and handwork are rewarding in themselves and have produced seafaring craft that are nothing less than works of art.

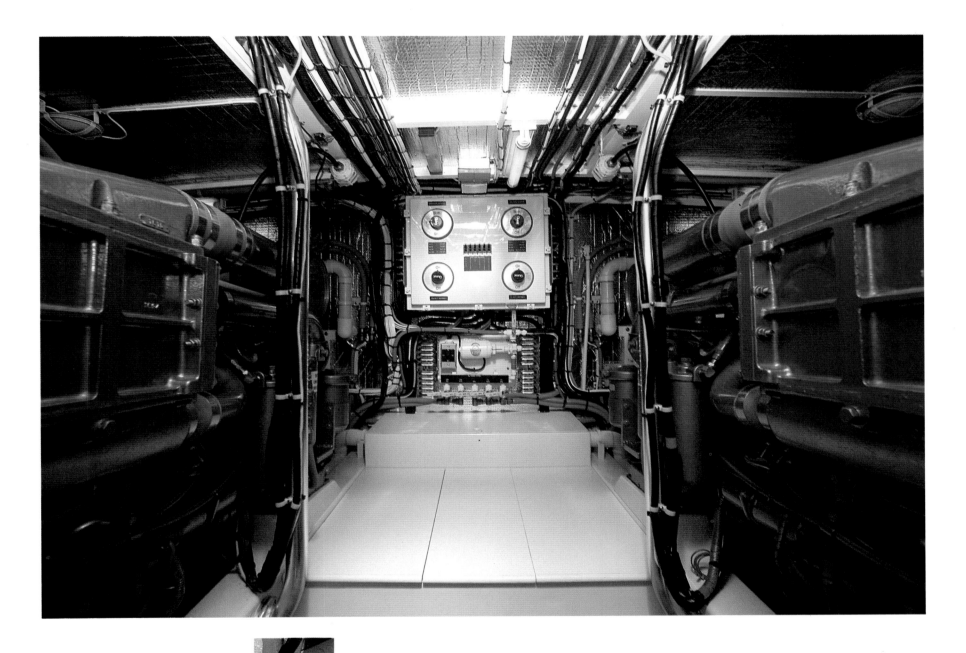

Power in design and propulsion are top priorities in offshore fishing yachts. The classic flared lines of this Rybovich and the semi-planing hulls of these big boats are served mightily by twin turbo diesel engines that can deliver speeds up to sixty knots.

Few words carry more magic to an offshore angler than "Fish on."

HENRY'S MARLIN

The dawn came clear, surprisingly clear, Henry Mitchell would remember. The air was crisp, with none of the brooding threat of the past couple of days when showers peppered Kauai's north shore and the sea rose up to remind him that he was, indeed, in the middle of the Pacific in winter. The winter of 1981, to be specific, and that morning Henry performed the ablutions that have forever marked the rising moments of fishermen: In the half-light, he eased up from beside his wife, Hollis, who stirred and said good-bye and good luck. Then, careful not to wake sleeping six-month-old Caitlin, he dressed and left his hotel room.

Outside, the brightening hospitality of the cloudless sky buoyed him, enriching that time at the beginning of a fishing day when the joy of anticipation can make children of us. The hours to come are still full of promise, and our reels sing in our heads to the pull of big fish. Had Henry known then how this fishing trip arranged by chance — no, by miracle — the day before would end, he would have been singing anthems out loud or perhaps cheering as he drove his rented car to the sandy mouth of the Hanalei River.

Henry Mitchell and I got to know each other over the conference tables of fisheries management politics in Alaska. He is now a member of the North Pacific Council, one of six such panels that govern the offshore fisheries of the United States. Henry's a lawyer, and for ten years, he's been the leading advocate for the aboriginal fishing rights of Indians and Eskimos of the western villages in the face of booming commercial development.

We really became friends, though, fly-fishing

from a canoe on a little stocked lake near his home in Anchorage, where he first told me the story of his marlin. He is given to telling the story if you even hint that you'll listen, but that, you'll agree when you've heard it, is forgivable. And he is, after all, a fisherman.

"The first fishing I remember was with my dad when I was five," Henry says between bites of scrambled eggs on another winter morning in Anchorage, after he has agreed to tell the long version for my tape recorder. "I was born in Cleveland and raised in Massachusetts. We used to do a lot of farm-pond fishing for largemouth bass and bluegills, and we'd also go over to Lake Erie to catch pike, right about the time the fishing was starting to fall off because of pollution. It was still good, though, and I remember going out and trolling. The favorite lure was called a Lazy Ike.

"Some of my best experiences with my father were when we'd take fishing vacations. That's a big part of why I fish—that and the challenge of the unknown. You go out and you're doing your best to catch something and you don't really know if you're going to succeed or not. I like all kinds of fishing, but I'd only ever dreamed of catching a marlin," he says. "You know, you start reading all these fishing magazines, and you pick up these books by Mc-Clane and Hemingway, and you try to put yourself in their place.

"That time in 1981 was my first trip to Hawaii, and I sort of thought, well, I'll take some fishing rods and maybe think about going out on a charter. I didn't really have the money, but I'd heard about the great billfishing, about the big fish, even though it's not really Kauai, but the Big Island for most of it."

For twenty-five years, thanks in large part to the appearance of the modern jet airliner, the Hawaiian archipelago—in particular, the Kona coast on the island of Hawaii—has been the locus for some big-time marlin and tuna fishing. Though fishing is still remarkably good, catches have fallen off due to heavy pressure from the mid-Pacific longline and driftnet fleets of Japan and other Asian countries.

There is an elemental conflict in issues such as sport fishermen versus commercial fishermen and the conservation practices of different nations. What, for instance, do I do when your revered culture threatens my revered culture and vice versa? The Japanese have almost no tradition of sport fishing in the sea. They have depended on the sea for food for tens of centuries, and now Americans are telling them that they have to stop catching marlin for food because we want to do it for sport. In 1989, the United States unilaterally banned commercial catching of marlin and prohibited sales of imported marlin. Whether other nations follow suit remains to be seen.

"Anyway," Henry Mitchell says, "I was over there on Kauai, and every day I'd take my fishing rods and walk around and the water would look great. But the only thing I'd catch were teeny multicolored reef fish and needle fish that were maybe three pounds. I remember thinking, 'If only I had a boat.' Then I saw Bill Hamilton.

"One afternoon, I was down at the mouth of the Hanalei River at a little state beach. A few people kept eighteen- to twenty-two-foot boats there. You really couldn't have anything bigger because the river ends in a shallow sandbar. I was just hanging around, looking at the water, and I ran into this guy who was fooling around on one of those 1950s outboard, semicabin cruisers, you know, with the fins on the back. He was cleaning some bonita when I came on him, and so I started talking with him, 'Where'd you catch them?' this and that.

"He was a kind of sun bum I guess, real laid-back. So I asked him, 'Hey, do you ever take people out?' And he

"They were a few miles away, and I remember thinking, 'Oh, the sharks will be back before they get here to help, and there'll be more of them.' I was horrified to think that this fish could be eaten out there and I didn't have a camera with me, and I was scared no one would ever believe me. I was tired but excited. I remember that boat coming. I could see it coming over the swells doing maybe fifty miles an hour, and I was sitting there looking for the sharks. And then the boat was there with three guys in it, and the marlin was dead.

"The guys were afraid to jump over to our boat in the swell because of the sharks. Finally, two of them jumped in, and the four of us were able to lift the marlin up and in. We put some ropes around it and tightened them up and grabbed the ropes and heaved it into the boat. It took up the whole boat.

"We sat there and had a beer, and one of them said, 'Well, who caught it?' And Bill said with pride, pointing to me, 'He did. He did real good.' I told Bill he should buy some new equipment, a new boat, and he said yeah, if he could catch a fish like this every day he'd buy a new boat.

"When we got back to the beach on the river, the word spread really fast. Within ten minutes, there were, like, a hundred people there. I didn't have a camera, and Bill said, 'We've got to get this fish to market,' and I said, 'Well, I've got to show my wife.' He said okay, so I jumped into the car and drove five miles down this winding road. I got to the hotel and said, 'Hollis, Hollis, I caught the biggest fish I ever saw.' Caitlin was taking a nap, and Hollis said, 'Yeah, yeah.' I finally got her and the baby into the car, and we ran back there and took some pictures. By that time, they'd cut it open and taken two or three big tuna out of it.

"I remember this old Hawaiian man asking Bill where he got it and Bill said off such-and-such a reef. The old man said, 'Yeah, lots of marlin there, but no one has ever landed one off that reef because of the white tips.'

"We took the pictures, and then Bill put the fish in the back of his Jeepster and took it to town. When he left, he said, 'Listen, Henry, any time you're back here you can go fishing for free. You did a pretty good job.'"

Henry showed me the pictures, and one of them is fixed forever in my mind. In it is a great fish on a beach, a magnificent blue and black and silver billfish, belly down as though swimming on the sand. Next to the fish, a rather ordinary looking middle-aged man is down on one knee, a baby cradled in his arms, an expression of astonished glee on his face. There can be no doubt who caught the marlin.

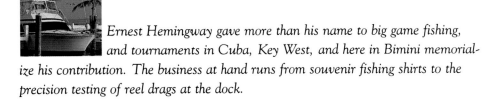

Ernest Hemingway gave more than his name to big game fishing, and tournaments in Cuba, Key West, and here in Bimini memorialize his contribution. The business at hand runs from souvenir fishing shirts to the precision testing of reel drags at the dock.

During nine tournament weeks a year, Bimini glistens with the most exotic expressions of boats, tackle, and high living anywhere. The rest of the time the fishing is still fabulous for blue marlin, sailfish, and the rest, and relaxed barely begins to describe life on the island whose name has become synonymous with big game fishing on the Atlantic. When Hemingway, Zane Grey, and Michael Lerner discovered this jewel just a chip shot off the Florida coast, they knew they'd found a fisherman's home.

Leaving the harbor in the morning, especially during a tournament, is the big game angler's moment of promise. Every possible preparation has been made; fuel, bait, food, and gear are aboard. Uncertainties about weather and the fish remain, but you know this is your day.

This sailfish won the Bimini Hemingway in 1990 for angler Jim Sutton, whose day turned out just as he hoped it would. The fish isn't a giant; the Atlantic record for sails is almost three times its weight, but smiles don't have to go into the IGFA (International Game Fish Association) book. Sailfish are the most common of the big game billfish, and except off the most populated coasts, stocks are in fairly good condition. Still, we know little about them, and major research is underway with tetracycline tagging and release to determine age and migratory patterns.

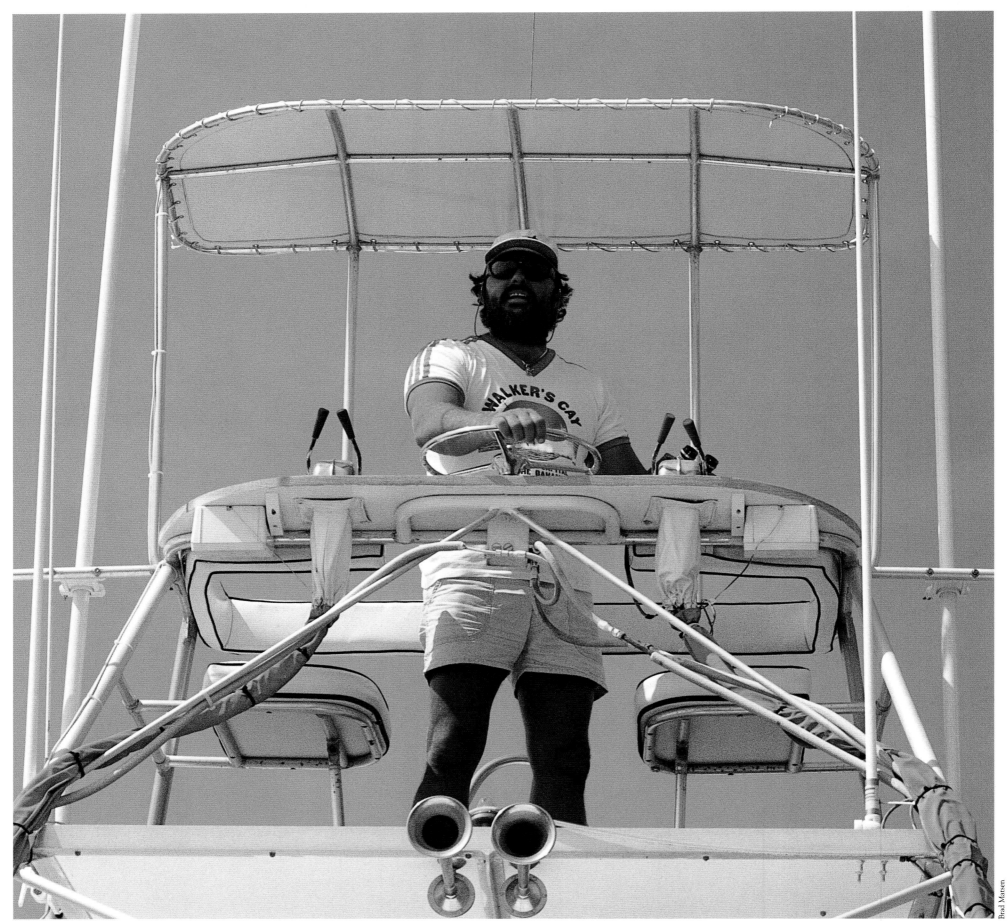

Captain Billy Black aboard the Duchess, *just after a marlin hook-up.*

MOTHER, MOTHER OCEAN

Billy Black was raised by his grandparents in Madison County at the western edge of the Okefenokee Swamp, where he started guiding when most kids his age were in first grade. For three dollars, his grandfather would let fishermen on his property; Billy would charge an extra dollar to show them where the bass and bluegill were thickest. Some nights he led alligator hunters, who favored the sparsely populated region that barely clings to its designation as dry land, where rivers like the Suwannee, the Alapaha, and the Withlacoochee spread the waters of the Appalachian drainage through the flats on their way to the sea. If the Atlantic were to rise but a couple of feet, southern Georgia and the entire peninsula we call Florida would join the great banks of the continental shelf beneath the surface of the ocean.

When he was seventeen, in 1962, Billy fol-

lowed the water to the sea, leaving the farm for the more expansive and adventurous environs of Sarasota on the central Florida Gulf Coast. There, live-baiting along the barrier islands that guard Sarasota Bay, he caught his first big fish, a sailfish, from a boat named *Easy Rider*. A year later, he graduated from high school and moved south and east to Hollywood on the edge of the Miami sprawl, where he fished from headboats until he joined the Air Force. If you ask him, Billy Black will tell you that he doesn't much care to talk about the Air Force or Vietnam, but he will admit to a longing for the ocean off Florida while he was away and to the sadness that implies for a man so far from home.

On the morning he is slipping around on the surfaces of his personal life for me, we are eating smoked marlin, bagels, sweet onions, and cream cheese in the air-conditioned salon of his *Duchess*, a twenty-two-year-old, fifty-foot Hatteras of supreme pedigree. Billy has the aplomb of a southern gentleman, his light drawl carrying a background hum of courtesy-but-no-nonsense and a definite sense of privacy. He is a solid-looking man with a two-speed face; it's either on or off, and sometimes the way he switches back and forth lets you know that control is a consideration in everything he does. And that is as it should be. What his clients have asked him to do for almost fifteen years is to bring their dreams to life — to catch big fish.

He is married to Theresa who is with us in the salon this morning in the slip at Walker's Cay, waiting for the clients. Billy and Theresa met in 1984 when she arrived at Walker's Cay as the mate aboard a Striker fishing yacht, her wanderings of ten years on the sea having led her to that moment and to him. Theresa, too, has worked on boats since leaving high school in Fort Lauderdale, and she is extremely capable in her dealings with big fish and clients, not to mention Captain Billy Black. At the cabin door, nose to the crack and the fresh morning air, is their dog, Huggie Bear, a thigh-size spaniel trained over the years to come alert to the words "Where are the porpoise?"

Billy's route to his fine situation as the number one captain at one of the world's best fishing resorts took him from Florida to the Lesser Antilles, then back up the Bahamian archipelago to its northernmost island, Walker's Cay. After Nam, he got his Coast Guard license to charter, then kicked around out of Port Everglades and the Keys, lobstering and chartering dive trips with a twenty-six-foot, single-screw launch. Life was good: Jimmy Buffett was singing about "Changes in Latitude, Changes in Attitude," and the yoke of authoritarian attitudes was being thrown off by young people all over America.

It was more than just a party, though, more than just dropping out. There were some casualties; drugs, alcohol, and bad calls claimed a few, Billy not among them. Instead, he was infected with the astonishing freedom of an age when, if he took the risk, he wouldn't have to languish in the quiet desperation of working for somebody else and balancing his checkbook in a suburb. "Most of all," he tells me, "I had to stay on the ocean. I love to fish."

Billy found the *Duchess* (she was named *Valor* then) in Grenada and managed to put together enough front money to become her owner. He started booking charters in the Caribbean, becoming an expert with using kites for fishing sailfish and refining his already thorough understanding of the other big game fish. In 1974, his clients broke both the men's and women's world records for yellowfin tuna on 20-pound test line, then at 177 pounds and 134 pounds, respectively. A charter captain's stock-in-trade is his reputation, and Billy was soon recognized as the real thing. At the time, the big fish charter world was an even tighter community than it is now, and the word spread about this intense ocean cowboy from Madison County: Billy Black catches fish.

Among the people who heard about Billy Black was a big, friendly man named Robert Abplanalp who, during the tumultuous years of the late 1960s and early 1970s, was as much an insider in the American culture as Billy was an outsider. Abplanalp, twenty years Billy's senior, invented and earned patents on an inexpensive seven-part valve that made aerosol spray possible. He owns the company, Precision Valve, lock, stock, and barrel. He made millions and emerged as a quiet philosophical and financial force in Republican politics. Abplanalp became one of Richard Nixon's best pals after the Kennedy election when, in what I understand was vintage Abplanalp in its directness and understatement, he wrote Nixon and said something like "Let me know if I can ever help."

The two met, Nixon's firm became the lawyers for

Abplanalp and Precision Valve, and they liked each other. Abplanalp became an intimate of America's most powerful politician and successfully avoided the noxious business of celebrity status by guarding his privacy, especially when it came to relaxing with Nixon. Right about this time, Abplanalp — by all accounts just one hell of a nice, very rich family man — ran headlong into the seductive vortex of big game fishing.

In 1968, Mr. A bought the leases to the northernmost group of islands in the Bahamas (a dozen in all), including Walker's, Grand, and Seal cays. Walker's already had a solid reputation among big game fishing aficionados as deluxe and very productive. More world records had been set by fishermen from Walker's Cay than by those from any other resort. With an airstrip and first-class accommodations, the hundred-acre wrinkle in the Bahamian shoals is a piece of heaven for anglers.

Walker's Cay is on the northeast edge of a subsea feature known as the Abaco Wall, a precipice over which the water depth tumbles from 90 to 3,000 feet to become the domain of big fish. Tuna, sailfish, wahoo, dolphin, white marlin, and blue marlin feast year-round on plankton, flying fish, mackerel, and, often, on each other.

"I answered an ad in 1977," Billy says. "Mr. A checked me out and said I was his captain. He's a great man, a nice man." So for the past thirteen years, Billy Black has been delivering the goods at Walker's Cay, performing a transformation on hundreds of anglers who arrive as normal human beings and who leave having touched the thunder of the great sea creatures. For this privilege, his clients pay six hundred dollars per day, which includes the *Duchess,* Billy and his mate, a Bahamian named Cardinal, plus all rods, reels, lures, and other tackle. The *Duchess* is pure Hatteras sport fisherman, one of the best all-around production boats in history, roomy and luxurious, powered by twin Detroit 871 diesels.

Running a big game charter boat is not a get rich quickly — or even slowly — lifestyle. "I don't have any complaints," Billy tells me. "But it's impossible to get to the point where you're making money while you're sleeping. It goes one year to the next, some years you get ahead, then you're back down again; something breaks and you fix it and it costs a lot of money, so you never really get ahead enough to invest."

Billy, like many top charter captains, is trying to put his reputation to work for him by producing his own line of trolling lures called Flash Dancers. They are particularly suited to the kind of high-speed trolling that has worked so well for Billy off Walker's. In those waters, he has brought about four hundred marlin to the boat over the years and hooked up with hundreds more. His biggest blue marlin ever — caught, tagged, and released in the summer of 1987 — he estimates went 850 pounds; his biggest brought to the dock set the current women's Bahamian record for 80-pound line at 694 pounds.

He also invented and patented a heavy-duty de-hooker, a simple but ingenious device that allows the angler or mate to release a fish with as little danger to all parties as possible. "If you don't have to worry about getting a hook in your hand, you're more likely to release the fish," he tells me. "It's a conservation tool as much as anything else."

Conservation of big game fish is a cause célèbre at Walker's Cay — a theme insisted on by Robert Abplanalp and his son, John, who is increasingly active in management of family affairs. In a move that many resort owners would have considered suicidal, Abplanalp raised the blue marlin minimum weight limit for the annual Walker's Cay tournament from 200 to 300 pounds in 1989. The decision took Walker's out of its previously dominant position as one of six stops on the circuit for the Bahamas Billfish Championship, since the other five resorts were not ready to make the dramatic gesture themselves. Walker's also leads the way in promoting catch, tag, and release in tournaments and in recreational fishing.

Abplanalp's rationale for raising the weight limit is easy to understand: Though we know very little about the life cycle of marlin, most ichthyologists agree that females do not spawn for the first time until they weigh over 200 pounds. "In 1976, they killed everything," I had been told by Monty Lopez, a fisheries biologist and director of The Billfish Foundation, a major conservation society. His vigorous promotion of billfish science and responsible fishing practices is legendary, and he got his message across loud and clear to Abplanalp.

And on the *Duchess* in the early spring of 1989, with the clear Bahamian morning light ricocheting off darting, squawking gullies, the clients arrive. Theresa stows the private supply of smoked marlin in the refrigerator, and Captain Billy Black is open for business. For three days, he will tend the hopes of a party of lawyers from South Carolina, including the senior partner, in his fifties, and his son, pushing thirty, their pilot, and several associates who will rotate into the daily lineup of four anglers on the *Duchess*. They board as Cardinal finishes icing the cooler.

If you caught fish every time you tried, you'd call it catching instead of fishing. Billy has told me that never has a client gotten angry or ugly-spirited about days fishing with no fish, but the pressure of expectation is palpable as the lawyers settle in. These are substantial men, clearly big dogs in their hometown, at least on the surface, because of the accoutrements of their lives: the private plane in which they arrived, the expensive sporting clothes, the polite but firm demeanor of people used to getting their own way. The anglers talk to Theresa and move gingerly about the boat stowing gear and fairly vibrating in anticipation as Billy, steering from the flying bridge, eases the *Duchess* out of her slip.

At sea, Billy is transformed from a friendly, slightly distracted fisherman at rest into a fully alert hunter. Once into blue water, at the loran numbers where he raised a big fish the week before, he directs Cardinal in setting the seven lines: a long rigger, a short rigger, and a flat line on the right and left sides, with a center rigger off the flying bridge. On deck, Cardinal moves like a chef, with little wasted motion, as he sets out the lures — the yellow-green imitating dolphin, the blue-white flying fish, and the black-gold yellowfin tuna — all the prey of blue marlin. Billy fishes only lures — Flash Dancers — because fewer fish die when released from lures, which most often hook their mouth, than from baits, which are swallowed.

The contrast is extreme between Billy and Cardinal, who work with a certainty at these tasks, and the clients, who fidget like children. The lawyers are determining the chair order: Each of the four will sit in the fighting chair, ready for a strike, for a half-hour. They will fish from about nine to three, giving each man three shots at the fighting chair on each of the three days they've booked the *Duchess*. The lures are now set, popping in a carefully laid pattern behind the *Duchess*, trailing intense streams of bubbles known as smoke. Billy fine-tunes the lures, but he and Cardinal have been working together for years and know each other's minds so few words pass. Over the rumble of the engines, Billy signals Cardinal by whistling through his teeth — stalking hunters make the same sound in the woods.

Billy's theory on catching marlin has a lot to do with covering large areas of the ocean at the relatively high speed of eight or nine knots, finding the proper water temperature — at this time of year about 78 to 80°F — and reading the tide rips, feeding birds, and baitfish. The combination is not unusual, but what Billy sells is his ability to tie these things together with his own urge to catch fish. Few anglers who charter big game boats and skippers could possibly catch fish by themselves.

The moment comes suddenly, always suddenly, and the appearance of prey bonds the anglers and crew together on a high-voltage circuit. Usually, it is Billy who first spots a fish, calling the location of the strike to Cardinal—right long, right short, or wherever. The angler in the chair takes the rod and reel, one of the big Penn 130s or the lighter 80s, and gets set to hit the fish, to set the hook.

Once the angler is prepared in the chair, Cardinal reels in the other lines. The rest of the clients press back against the cabin bulkhead or station themselves on the flying bridge for the overhead view. Theresa is on deck now, calmly but firmly telling the angler what to do. Most of the time, the angler is only marginally familiar with the business of coming fast to a fish weighing hundreds of pounds. Huggie Bear crouches in a corner by the door, and two hundred yards astern, the marlin breeches, fighting free of the water to challenge the hook and this terrible intrusion on her domain. (All big marlin are females.) The lawyers are cheering—literally cheering—and the youngest of them, who happens to be the one in the chair, takes a strain against the fish.

Billy Black watches from above and directs the action, confident and alert in the extreme, handling the boat in a rhythm with the fish and the angler. The fights are long, sometimes hours long, and they have acts and stages of varying character. The angler rests, tires. The marlin sounds, holding firm straight down under the boat, then runs and leaps again and again to shed the ocean's safety in its anger and fright, in its desire to escape.

As the fish is brought to the boat, Billy leaves the flying bridge and tends to the de-hooking. It is the angler's choice to release the fish or not. Most often they do aboard the *Duchess*, Billy first marking the marlin with a dart and tag so that its migratory patterns can be traced if it is ever caught again. The information on the fish and the tag is recorded on a postcard and mailed to a fisheries center. And then it is over, the fish gone back to the deep, the anglers celebrating with handshakes, cheering, back-slapping. Though the one who caught the fish is shining the brightest, they are all—including Billy—fully revealed in their excitement, absolutely unprotected by the normal veneers of identity and personality.

After a few minutes of this, Billy retreats to his flying bridge, nudges the *Duchess* into gear, and slides a cassette into the tape player. He turns to look down on the continuing glee below him and whistles to Cardinal who begins setting out the lines. Then, as though the moment of the catch has come into his mind again, he punches the air in an athlete's victory salute and, from deep inside, says out loud, "All right. All right." The control is gone; pure pleasure has visited the captain.

 Bimini is the home of Hemingway's fictional painter, Thomas Hudson, in his last book, Islands in the Stream, and by implication, the author's spiritual residence as well. Fishermen, pirates, and mariners of every stripe have also been inspired by this horseshoe-shaped atoll that rises from the Great Bahama Bank less than fifty miles east of Miami. Bimini is like a base camp in the Gulf Stream, hence its reputation for big and plentiful blue marlin. For the land-bound, Bailey Town and Alice Town offer a taste of the best in Bahamian hospitality.

It takes about thirty seconds to get used to the sand floor at the
End of the World Bar, the lore of the Bimini Big Game Fishing
Club, and the Bimini Blue Water Resort. In the 1930s, Papa hung out at The
Compleat Angler, the oldest inn on the island, which now features a collection of
Hemingway memorabilia.

Bimini is still just one big fishing camp, but lay days when you stay ashore bring the pleasures of sleepy afternoons, beach time, diving, or a ramble through the Straw Market for the inevitable trinkets. The evenings and nights are so good on Bimini, it's a wonder anyone ever leaves.

 Among the most compelling truths about offshore big game angling is that it gets you to some of the most beautiful and varied places on earth. The twenty-minute plane ride from downtown Miami to Bimini, for instance, is a time machine to another world. And of course, there is always the sea itself.

Outbound from Bimini, ready for the hunt during the Ernest Hemingway Tournament.

THE SWORDFISH & THE LADY

O ff Rhode Island, the shimmer of morning above brings the big female swordfish to feed near the surface after a night in the depths. She works in the blackness on schools of mackerel and bluefish that are chasing feed downward in the vertical rhythm of light and dark. She moves with impossible grace and speed, the sea flowing over her smooth, scaleless body, perfectly shaped for what I like to think of as water-flying. Her cornflower blue eyes are enormous, the size of salad plates and best suited for the dim reflections of the abyss; the brightness of day is startling. She undulates constantly, transforming the power of her long muscles into motion and allowing her eyes and the sensors of her lateral line to sweep a wide arc in search of food. She is pure hunter, an apex predator when mature, a meal only for humans and the largest sharks.

Her life is a matter of moving and feeding and breeding, with no magnificence created from within, no self-awareness of her majesty; it seems odd that she is almost certainly incapable of thoughts of elegance or simple purpose or joy. In the spring, though, she spawned, squeezing clouds of eggs into the fertile gyre of the Sargasso Sea (perhaps) where a male unknown to her completed the miracle with his milt. Then, thin and haggard after the difficult, hungry season of giving birth, she made her way a thousand miles north, tracking the warm currents of the Gulf Stream to the subsea plains and canyons of the Northwest Atlantic.

Now, her prey rise from the depths on summer days in the relative shallows off Rhode Island, and so she follows. Around her, the water crackles with the intensity of light's visitation, alive with the splashes of diving birds, and the flash of dustlike plankton with its collectively blazing presence. The amazing chorus lines of mackerel seem to be of common mind when thousands of them turn to flee in perfect harmony during her attack. Some she stuns with her bill and returns to filter them through her toothless mouth and into the pressurized engine that is her gut. That is all.

From the human perspective, though, she is a glorious masterpiece of the ocean, this fish of power and mystery. The broadbill swordfish, *Xiphias gladius*, is the only member of its taxonomic family; no other animal participates in the zoological symphony in quite the same way. This one — this 450-pound female cruising on the surface in the flat morning light off the coast of Rhode Island — is about thirteen feet long from her tail to the tip of the flat, hard, ebony-colored bill that accounts for one-third of her length. Her dorsal fin is deeply concave on its trailing edge and permanently erect, unlike those of the marlins and sailfish that fold into a slit in the body when they swim at speed.

As the day warms she continues to rise, finally breaking the chrome sheet of the surface with her dorsal fin and the upper half of her tail. The day is calm, and she presents an image unlike any other sea creature, leaving subtle twin ripples in her wake and flashing patterns in the sun that have no equal. Some students of the swordfish suggest that such basking encourages digestion of the night's heavier ration of food; some say there is simply better hunting on the surface in daylight — but no one knows for sure why this moment of vulnerability occurs. Regardless, a fisherman who beholds a swordfish on the surface never forgets the first time.

And on this day, July 5, 1959, Nancy Nye Wilder hears her captain beside her on the flying bridge call out "Over there," pointing as he cranks his thirty-two-foot Brownell, *Surfmaster III*, into a tight bank to approach the fish. According to plan rather than practice — for this is the first swordfish they have ever baited — Nancy bolts down the ladder to the deck, removes the rigged squid from a cooler, and hurls it into the wake of the boat. She then checks her equipment, the rod, the line on the reel, the condition of the deck around her, all the while keeping an eye on her prey. The fish swings past the stern quarter as the *Surfmaster III* rumbles through an arc to bring the bait to the basking giant. And then she waits.

Nancy and her captain, Bud Phillips, have a deal. Both are from Little Compton, a quiet village on the eastern sliver of Rhode Island where New England dissolves into the Atlantic in a chorus of boulders, hardscrabble beaches, and surf known as Sakonnet Point. For centuries, day-boaters and summer people have come from Newport and Providence and Boston to Little Compton for holidays. The countryside is pastoral, woven throughout with low stone walls perfectly crafted from the glacial till that underlies the fertile soil, and the weather in the summer season is a charming combination of foggy mornings and hot afternoons.

More than anything else, though, the place is cherished for the fishing, and it is in that pursuit that Nancy and Bud became friends. She was, as she says, "doing mostly striped bass and some bluefish," when Bud suggested swordfish. He had been running charters out of Sakonnet Point since his youth when he discovered he could make more money as a charter skipper than as a purely commercial fisherman, which was his calling for awhile. Bud is a big, handsome man, given to enthusiasm and invigorated by the joy of doing just what he wants to with his life. In the winter, he taught skiing in Vermont.

Deciding to take the *Surfmaster III* offshore was a bit of a reach for Bud. She was a fine boat, but with only a single engine and the rudimentary electronics of the

1950s, he had to navigate—often in fog—by dead reckoning, water temperature, and water color to make his way to the Gulf Stream eddy that sets up each summer off Rhode Island. Nancy had been chartering Bud and the *Surfmaster III* every Tuesday for some time, but they had never been offshore until the summer of 1959. The boat had a fifteen-foot pulpit on the bow, which meant that Bud could harpoon swordfish (the common commercial method) as well as bait them with rod and reel for sport. According to his deal with Nancy, they would try to bait the fish they found, but if the fish refused to strike, Bud would harpoon it for market. If they got a fish either way, Nancy didn't pay for the charter; if not, she paid. And they also chased white marlin and tuna as part of the bargain.

On this morning of the first swordfish, though, all the history and the arrangements and the details pale in the brilliance of the moment when the sea explodes forty yards behind the boat and Nancy hooks up with a broadbill swordfish. Nothing would ever be the same for "Nannie" Nye Wilder, a Boston doctor's daughter, braced on the deck of the *Surfmaster III*, setting the hook with the fierce certainty of a born hunter. There she is, a compact blonde on the threshold of middle age, wearing a blue pullover that matches the eyes of the unseen swordfish, with Bud shouting instructions and the reel screaming. From that moment, Nancy would be as bound to the broadbill swordfish as most of us are bound to our families.

Most of what happened during the battle has blurred a bit now for both Nancy and Bud, but there was joy and laughter and pain. She fought the swordfish standing up the whole time, since the *Surfmaster III* did not have a fighting chair, and she suffered mightily. From the first long run after the strike, the fish moved steadily seaward forcing Bud to chase it with the boat. They saw the fish

only briefly, but long enough to know it was in the 400- to 500-pound range—a great fish. The reel core showed many times as the fish sounded and ran deep, eventually covering tens of miles from the 26-fathom to the 32-fathom lines on the grounds local fishermen know as the Little Fingers.

And then, after four and a half hours, her arms and legs and back screaming with the fire of tortured muscles, Nancy felt the fish leave her. She knew the numbing truth of the slack line. "I felt as if I had lost a friend, a true friend," she would tell me later in her living room at Little Compton. Nancy is seventy now, and she is reading her recollections of her first swordfish from a sheet of yellow notepaper, cues she has prepared as a hedge against the lapses brought by a stroke fifteen years ago. Whatever that vagrant turn of health took from her, nothing of the life-force is missing from Nancy Wilder.

Bud Phillips is here. Now in his sixties, long and lean and stretched out in his chair, wearing a green-and-white-checked shirt, rust-colored trousers, and boat shoes with no socks, his face is lit by an expression of constant amusement. The man just loves fishing. And David Cornell is with us, too. David and his brother Chris worked as deckhands for Bud during the summers of their teenage years in Little Compton.

So Nancy finishes telling me what she wrote down to make sure I get the important parts of her life with swordfish. Then, with the help of her onyx-head cane, she stands and beckons me to a chart on the bare-wood wall of the room. As we walk slowly to it, I glance at the brass plate below the mounted striped bass over the fireplace and see that the fish weighed 43½ pounds when Nancy caught it on the last day of the local fishing festival to win first prize and a measure of local fame. I see, too, the silver-capped swordfish bills hanging near her desk and the award pennant from the Cuttyhunk Swordfish Tournament. And there's a mounted white marlin, 59 pounds, caught by her daughter, Sarah (known as "Spook"), who started fishing as a child with her mother.

Nancy's fishing log book, which she showed me before Bud arrived and we started talking a lot, contains her notes on many seasons of successful offshore fishing, including the day Spook took that particular marlin: "August 6, 1962—Offshore Bud; Terry, Spook, Gusty Hornblower, NNW (Nancy Nye Wilder); White marlin bonanza on light tackle, 20-lb. test mono; NNW released 85–95 lb., 50 jumps in 30 minutes; Spook boated 59 lb. and Gusty 59 lb.; No broadbill."

After a day like that, I say to Nancy, the thing I notice most is that you mention the lack of a swordfish, and she says, "That's all I really thought about out there after the first one." And then she is pointing to the chart, on which she has noted all her swordfish. It is a standard maritime navigation chart showing the bottom contours off Rhode Island and southern Massachusetts, waters that have been both hospitable and terrifying to Americans for over four hundred years. On Nancy's chart are constellations of dime-store stick-on stars in different colors, representing her fishing memories, and we stand there as she explains them to me. The green ones are white marlin, boated or released, and there are many of them, as there are blue ones for giant tuna. The chart is pocked with penciled Xs, too, dozens of them, which Nancy tells me are swordfish seen and harpooned. "They almost never take a bait," she says, with a plaintiveness in her voice that dissolves as she turns our attention to the red stars, swordfish she fought and lost. There, with the notation of the date, 7/5/59 (July 5, 1959), is the first one. "And these," she says, her chin tilted up because the chart is high on the wall, "these are the broadbills I caught, these silver

stars." They are in a cluster, due south of Martha's Vineyard around 41 degrees by 70 degrees 30 minutes, with the dates 8/12/60, 7/16/63, 8/12/63, and 8/10/66. Four of them.

Resorting to statistical comparison to tell you how remarkable it is that this vital woman beside me caught four broadbill swordfish on rod and reel doesn't do justice to the power of her experience. It is important to know, though, that only four or five hundred people, by the best estimates, have ever taken the broadbill on rod and reel while baiting it on the surface during daylight hours. This is not to denigrate the achievement of those who have since brought one to the boat by the more recent methods of fishing hundreds of fathoms deep, at night, using light sticks, and never seeing the fish until it is at the boat.

The first ever taken on rod and reel in daylight came off Santa Catalina Island, California, in 1913, when W. C. Boschen took a 355-pound broadbill. (They called it a marlin swordfish in those days.) The International Game Fish Association (IGFA) world record, which stands today, was set off Iquique, Chile, by Lou Marron who took a fish weighing 1,182 pounds. Much bigger fish have been harpooned, most from the waters of the South Atlantic and Pacific where the fish are bigger than they are in the North Atlantic. A 1,565-pound broadbill was brought to market in Chile. In 1921, a dressed fish was delivered at the Boston Fish Pier weighing 915 pounds; alive, it would have weighed 1,100 pounds.

The swordfish has seduced anglers for decades for many reasons other than size; for one thing, the odds against success are so enormous. The fascination with the species has also inspired some of the best scientific inquiry into the lives of big game fish, not the least of which is the work of Michael Lerner. Lerner, who began his fishing life off Long Island on a skiff with his father jigging for flounders, eventually influenced modern big game fishing more than any other single person. He founded the IGFA, the Lerner Lab in Miami, and several other conservation and research organizations; he set numerous records most often in company with his wife, Helen, and personally conducted landmark studies on the sea and its creatures. "Of all the men associated with the golden age of deep sea angling," wrote George Reiger in his wonderful book *Profiles in Saltwater Angling*, "the name of Michael Lerner looms the largest."

And Lerner was absolutely smitten by swordfish. The difficulty in finding and catching so exotic a creature was part of his passion, and he shared it with contemporaries Ernest Hemingway, Kip Farrington, and Alfred Glassell, Jr., who, with due respect to the other great game fish, acknowledged the supremacy of the swordfish. Lerner himself actually landed two in a single day off South America, and Helen Lerner has the distinction of becoming the first woman angler to take a broadbill on both the Atlantic and Pacific oceans.

But Michael Lerner was a scientist, and so the mysteries of the broadbill's migration, life cycle, and biology drove his most enduring work. He led numerous expeditions during the 1930s and 1940s to gather basic information on the swordfish, because there were absolutely no data at the time. Lerner realized, as do many of us now, that without better understanding of the swordfish and other big game fish, we will likely decimate the species.

The swordfish has also borne the burden of a booming commercial fishery, which has now reduced the likelihood of taking a broadbill in daylight on the Northwest Atlantic to absolute zero, and by any other method to a rarity. Most of the action in the North Atlantic grounds is on tuna and the occasional white marlin in the canyons between New Jersey and Long Island. In 1989, the managers of the fisheries in U.S. waters realized the broadbill's

plight and all but eliminated the commercial quota.

It is impossible to consider the gleam in Nancy Wilder's eyes as we stand in her house in Little Compton without the understanding that those days are history. Bud leaves his chair and walks to the chart, where Nancy and I are still talking about her swordfish, about her victory in the Cuttyhunk tournament, and about how, in 1971, they folded the tournament because no swordfish had been caught for two years, and very few since.

Bud charters inshore now, mostly for bluefish, striped bass, and sharks, although occasionally he'll run a boat for another owner who wants to go offshore for marlin. He hasn't seen a broadbill for years. "I don't know what it is about swordfish," Bud says, "but it gets into your blood. Seeing one is like seeing a million of them. I don't think you'll ever be able to swordfish the way we did, though, and I'm glad we got in on it. They've been hit hard by the longlines and trawls. Who knows, maybe they'll come back if we let up on them."

Nancy Wilder still summers in Little Compton, but she doesn't fish any more. Right after her stroke, she learned one-handed fishing from a friend who'd lost his arm in the war, but she has pretty much retired from her grounds off Sakonnet Point. She and Bud still get together once in awhile, though, to talk about swordfish.

Offshore fishing at its best is a blend of careful preparation, the angler's desire to succeed, and the ability to instantly and properly react to the strike of a big fish. This 500-pound black marlin demands all of that, and more.

Though the strike is not always a billfish or giant tuna, it's hard to be disappointed when you land hard fighters like the roosterfish or the delicious neon show known as mahimahi, dolphin, or dorado. These were taken off Costa Rica.

Playing a billfish is a matter of patience, alertness, and in no small measure, physical strength and endurance. During the early years of offshore sport angling with rods and reels, it was not unusual for a fishing club to retain a physician to meet returning anglers at the dock. Even today, with the modern geared, adjustable drag reels and precision rods, anglers are actually injured fighting fish. In 1989, off Hawaii, a fisherman was pulled into the sea, fighting chair and all, by a giant marlin and towed down eighty feet before he was able to break free.

Usually, though, a well-hooked fish loses the fight. Since people began realizing that the populations of even the mighty are fragile, catch-tag-and-release fishing has become more common. Still, many marlin, like these, end up on dinner tables and walls.

Frank Johnson, king of the Soft Head lure, inventor, bon vivant, and teller of tall tales.

FRANK, THREE, & MONTY

Hunting attended the birth of Art; perhaps it might have been the obstetrician. —Roger Caras, *Death as a Way of Life*

"The real reason Hemingway didn't really like fishing in tournaments is because he couldn't stand losing," Frank Johnson says to me across a table of Cuba Libres and aromatic, spicy shrimp. Like almost every other bar in South Florida, this one has hatch-cover tables, blue-plastic marlin swizzle sticks in the drinks, and steel-drum music embroidered on the background hum of conversation. On the bench next to Frank, his son Frank Johnson III—known as "Three"—nods his head and peels a shrimp. He has been listening and playing straight man to his father's stories for thirty years or so, and he is a fan, a son who is a friend.

A lot of people are friends of Fast Frank. He's a tall, intense yet whimsical character, a raconteur and *bon vivant* who invents himself as he goes along. Frank and Three are big game fishermen of substantial repute, but they're also in the business of big fish, manufacturers of lures and rigging who enjoy not only financial success but a kind of celebrity status, too.

It's hard to get into a conversation about big game fishing with any older Gulf and Caribbean hand who doesn't at some point summon the romanticism of Hemingway, the boat *Pilar,* and the brave, true fish. Hemingway was master of the code of the hunter: grace under pressure. "He wasn't what you'd call a regular guy," Frank says, "but a lot of people have made a lot of money off what he wrote about fishing." And where we are, in that bar, is across the parking lot from the Coconut Grove convention center where Frank and Three and hundreds of other men and women in the big fish business have gathered to commit commerce on a grand scale.

Hemingway in full roar could not have imagined a Miami with a neon-trimmed freeway and thousand-foot buildings that change color against the night, or oceans in which big fish are in steady retreat from the press of the human population. He would have been surprised, I'm sure, by the proliferation of jet travel and its implications for big game fishing and by the power of mass media to deliver dreams of the exotic far more powerfully than his novels. He could not have envisioned the commerce that has grown up around what to him was an almost mystical undertaking set aside for the few people who could get to the fishing grounds via a long and expensive process. But whether he would have been offended by what was going on in the convention center's cavernous halls in the spring of 1989, he would have been interested.

I flew to Miami for the First World Exposition of Saltwater Fishing, because I sensed something akin to critical mass in such an assemblage of buyers and sellers; I knew that a governing generality about big fish and people would be revealed. I had prepared for the trip by accumulating facts on the business of big fish and had learned, for instance, that the number of Americans who fish in the ocean each year has grown from about 4.5 million in 1955 to about 16 million in 1989. Not all of them had gone offshore for the big game species, but even someone who has only plunked a bottom rig off a pier is a likely candidate to fish offshore for big fish at some time in his or her life. In 1955, those fishermen paid somebody—for a rod and reel, a boat, a charter, and so on—a total of about $500 million for the pleasure of fishing. By 1989, the take had soared to about $4 billion.

The money, of course, doesn't account for all the pieces of the cultural puzzle laid out before me as I walk from the muggy morning heat of South Florida into the air-conditioned exhibit hall. There, in a giant grid of carpeted aisles, are enterprises ranging from ten-foot-by-ten-foot shops with lures arranged on a table by a guy and his wife in Hawaiian shirts, to the flashy exhibits of aggressive, deep-pocket manufacturers, like Shimano Rods and Reels, that are making a strategic assault on the offshore fishing market.

In an entirely separate hall, my guidebook says, is the Marine Electronics Pavilion, home of wizardry like fish-finders, radar, and loran that makes the modern offshore fisherman an astonishingly formidable predator. And there's more. Outside, on the waterway adjacent to the exhibit halls, is a dock with about seventy boats on display, from twenty-foot outboards to a mind-bending ninety-foot sport fisherman called *That's My Hon* that will do fifty-two knots. The boats are uniformly seductive, with those rich-looking, blue, fitted-canvas covers over winches and equipment, gleaming aluminum towers and outriggers, and elegant hulls that speak of luxury and dominance in the face of the elements.

From the doors of the main hall, I am drawn into a current of people meandering past several hundred booths selling charter trips, magazines, fighting chairs with inlaid abalone trim, rods made before your eyes by third-generation craftsmen, clothing that ranges from the serious business of flotation gear to the whimsy of marlin belts and T-shirts with slogans like "The worst day of fishing beats the best day of work," gorgeous fish art, reels, line, and lures. And interspersed among them are the representatives of fishing advocacy groups such as the International Game Fish Association (IGFA), The Billfish Foundation, and the National Center for the Environment.

I keep moving, wanting to look at the whole show

before getting down to details, and I stick to my plan until I come across Frank and Three. Lures are probably the most volatile part of the big fish market for several reasons. They are the least expensive of the essentials (the others being rods, reels, and boats). They are relatively easy to manufacture, which attracts more small entrepreneurs. Lures are exotic in both design and purpose. And finally, more than any other single fishing product, they depend on reputation for success. While most lures either find a modest collection of devotees or disappear entirely, a hot lure fished successfully by a famous captain or angler can be a cash producer of the better mousetrap variety.

A pretty good crowd has beaten a path to Fast Frank's booth that day, which is why I stop for the first time in my Expo wandering. Gathered around a television set are maybe forty people watching a videotape of a man named Jerry Dunaway and his friend Deborah Maddux setting world records with Frank's lures. The latest and greatest of the lures is called the Hooker Red Bailey Soft Head, a combination of plastic and steel that, in the thumb-size brain of a billfish, translates into "easy meal."

Jerry Dunaway borrowed $150 and started an appliance rental company in Texas, built it up to national class, then sold out for $40 million a week before the oil crash a few years ago. Or so the story goes. Now he spends most of his time aboard his boat, the 48-foot *Hooker*, which he takes around the world aboard his self-contained 130-foot mother ship, the *Madam*. The IGFA awards men's and women's world records for different line strengths from 2 pounds to 130 pounds for the marlins, swordfish, and mako shark, and 2 pounds to 80 pounds for sailfish and tuna. No anglers, especially no man and woman team, have ever taken record chasing as seriously as Dunaway and Maddux; the 1989 IGFA record book shows their names fifteen times, mostly in the ultralight line classes.

Jerry and Deborah are here at the World Expo; in fact, they are standing right there with Fast Frank and Three and the rest of the crowd watching the television. I edge in and see Frank up close for the first time, working the crowd, pointing to action on the screen. Three seems to be the detail man, selling the steak while his father sells the sizzle, although Frank's manner is not one of a huckster. He likes people to catch on to his ideas and patiently explains rigging, the concepts of his lures, and fishing technique to all comers. He is eccentric, engaging, and given to unselfconscious bursts of enthusiasm. In articles like "The Sun Never Sets on a Softhead Lure," fishing writers who know Frank have described him as "an inventive genius."

I hang around watching Frank and Three and finally introduce myself to Frank who has been watching me watch him. Perhaps because of my notebook, he immediately includes me in his scene, in the action. I shake hands with Jerry and Deborah, watch the video again, and pick up bits of Frank's story.

"All you have to do is feel it," he says, handing me a Red Bailey. "See. It's soft. That's it. It feels more like flesh. It just fools the fish more." He tells me that the design is from Jerry and his captain on the *Hooker*, Skip Smith. Frank's company, Mold Craft, manufactures other plastic products, too, on most of which he holds patents, but his passion is fishing.

Our rambling conversation is interrupted frequently by Frank's friends and customers, most of whom are both. We slide from boats to gear to anthropology, and at one point, I ask Frank why there aren't more mounted fish or even pictures of hanging fish at the Expo. "Just about everybody tags and releases now," he says. "And one of the best things about lures that work this well is that you don't kill as many fish. It doesn't take a rocket scientist to realize that the fish aren't there as they were a few years ago. Go talk to Monty Lopez."

Monty Lopez is the director of The Billfish Foundation, a new but insistent voice in the outcry for protection of the fish. That night, he was over on Bimini giving the biggest trophy of a recent tournament to the angler who'd released the most fish. I was told he'd be around the next day.

After those drinks and shrimp with Frank and Three when the Expo closed, I wandered some more — this time restlessly along the central Miami waterfront, which had been given over to highly organized temples to shopping. There, among the buying and eating, I thought for the first time about the implications of a $4-billion industry fired by primal instincts but fed by a finite, fragile prey. None of these people goes to sea to kill a marlin, drag it back to the hut, and feed his or her family. But almost everyone who has ever hooked up with a big fish will tell you that the moment is one of absolute clarity, that there are no distractions, none of the mundane matters that infect ordinary life, and especially, no uncertainty of purpose. It had affected me powerfully, too, and after experiencing the high voltage among the buyers and sellers at World Expo, the entire matter of hunting big fish took on new shades of meaning.

Without a doubt, hunting is the master behavior pattern of the human species. I found a lot to read, but most of it boiled down to this: "Agriculture has dominated human existence for less than one percent of man's history," writes Roger Caras, in *Death as a Way of Life*, which I carried with me to Miami. "Man, it seems certain, became man during and because of his years as a hunting animal. If killing didn't feel good on some primal level, few would do it; if sexual intercourse felt like shaving,

there would be no population explosion."

And listen to Barry Lopez writing in *Arctic Dreams*: "The evidence is good that among all northern aboriginal hunting peoples, the hunter saw himself bound up in a sacred relationship with the larger animals he hunted. The relationship was full of responsibilities — to the animals, to himself, and to his family." And later, "the focus of a hunter in a hunting society was not killing animals but attending to the myriad relationships he understood bound him to the world he occupied with them."

What we do now with this powerful dose of the hunting juice is primarily symbolic and quite puzzling beyond the most banal quest for a thrill. Certainly, the complex of commerce and urgency about big game fishing could not have built up around simple thrill seeking. "We are interested," Caras writes, "in the phenomenon of men — particularly men, but some women, too, taking time off from essential economic activity to engage in the often strenuous and even dangerous task of killing animals for the sheer pleasure of doing it. Civilized man has lost the need but not the urge for the chase, the stalk, and the kill."

The problem with such symbolic activity and the booming commercial web we have woven around it is that modern human beings are quite capable of extinguishing not only a prey but a species. All of that can leave a fairly dark smear of pessimism on something like big game fishing, but I also learned at World Expo that we are on the case. Monty Lopez (no relation to Barry) was ordering a hot dog when I came across him the next day during my drift through the aisles. He is a dark, compact man in his thirties, the kind of guy who might have been an underweight but successful running back on the high school football team. We settled on a bench outside in the shade, enjoying a few minutes away from the activities of the hunt inside. "If it weren't for boat-show hot dogs, I wouldn't get anything to eat at all," he says. And then he told me about himself and The Billfish Foundation, non-stop, never taking another bite of the dog.

Monty Lopez, it turns out, is a former government fisheries biologist gone renegade. Born in Fort Worth, Texas, and bonded to the ocean in college in Corpus Christi, Monty went to work for the National Marine Fisheries Service as a game fish biologist in 1972. For the next seventeen years, he worked on solving the mysteries of marlin mostly, but game fish in general. Despite the lineage of scientific inquiry dating back to pioneer marine scientist Michael Lerner in the 1930s, not much is known about the big fish.

"We don't even know how old marlin are," Monty says. "We know that there aren't as many as there used to be, that all the middle-size fish are disappearing, that smaller fish are being caught. Until 1981, we had to hunt real hard to find a small marlin for research. Now they're everywhere. It's not good that we're catching small and big fish, but few in-between," he says. "We know that a marlin under two hundred pounds hasn't spawned, which is why we're getting a lot of tournaments to raise their weight limits, especially here in the Bahamas and the Gulf."

In its first year of existence, The Billfish Foundation has about a thousand members, anglers whose hunting philosophy is manifested in the graphics on the Foundation T-shirts: "How many will there be in 2001?" reads the slogan over a stylized marlin. "The trustees were just a bunch of guys who said, 'This is a good idea,'" Monty tells me. "Our number one goal is to draw sportsmen and scientists together, to encourage more science and conduct research ourselves. Catching, tagging, and releasing produces knowledge and keeps the fish in the water and that's what we're committed to. We're also a political

organization. We want to provide information on the basic economic value of billfishing to the United States and assess the attitudes of sport fishermen toward management. We have support from manufacturers, from fishermen, from scientists.

"Fishing is unique," Monty says, when I ask him why. "There are so many things you get out of fishing that don't have anything to do with catching the fish. People need recreation to remain sane. And as far as big fish go, we are human beings and we have evolved to the point where we are the number one predator on land; the blue marlin has evolved to the point of being the number one predator in the sea. It is this confrontation that big game fishermen seek and need, and we have the right to satisfy our desires responsibly.

"I hate to say this but in the old days, a lot of fishermen, a lot of famous fishermen, didn't really give a rat's ass if they killed everything that swam. But marlin are magic. Wouldn't you want your kid to catch one?"

About all I could do listening to Monty was sit there in the breeze, nod my head, and take notes. "If billfishing disappears," he says, "we're taking something away that is a dream. That's why I don't really represent the guy in the boat. I represent the fish."

The extravagances of craftsmanship and money lavished on offshore fishing boats are probably akin to the hunters' tribal respect for their prey. The beauty of the craft we use to chase big fish is functional, and in many situations lives will depend on the sure hand of the shipwrights or the careful maintenance of the crew. The business of building deep sea boats eliminates the shoddy and uncertain by reputation, and the dependable builders are elevated to legendary stature. This Merritt is a prime example of the art.

The fighting chair is the centerpiece on an offshore fishing boat. In it, an angler makes fast to a fish sometimes the size of a horse and often experiences hours of pain, exhilaration, and exhaustion. The chair cannot fail; it must swivel smoothly to face the fish and, with its footrest and harness, give the angler leverage to resist the pull of an animal fighting for its life. Fighting chairs are so central to the business of big game fishing that manufacturers usually embellish them and other deck gear with intricate totems of abalone or veneer, often in the form of billfish or tuna.

As the designs of offshore boats were refined, builders and owners expanded their art to include more than just the business side of getting to sea and back with reliable engines and controls. Modern sportfishers are true yachts, with elegant furnishings and appointments.

*Many own-
ers take ex-
tended cruises in the course
of hunting big fish aboard
their sport-fishing yachts,
and builders have responded
by creating fine homes-away-
from-home. Competition in
the boating market has produced an evolution of special
fabrics and materials that
can survive the marine environment, and most cruising
sportfishers feature climate-
controlled interiors and other
comforts. The days of Spartan conditions aboard boats
like Hemingway's famous
Pilar are gone forever, and
so are the men-only rules
that once held sway over
conditions afloat.*

Late in the day on the Costa Rican coast, Pacific side.

THE HONEYMOONERS

At Mazatlán, the sun rises over the continent to the east, casting the long shadows of wrinkled terrain across the harbor and the anchored sport-fishing fleet. Each tidy group of boats is marked by its owner's distinctive color, reminiscent of racing silks; the prideful reds, greens, and blues are alive in the young light on the estuary. On the charter docks, the scaffolds that held yesterday's marlin and sailfish are empty, with no remembrance of the fleet's return fifteen hours earlier. On a white wall behind the fish-weighing scale, I can just make out the carefully lettered motto of this particular charter outfit: THE WORST DAY FISHING IS BETTER THAN THE BEST DAY WORKING!

The boatmen seem to appear rather than arrive in the dim beginnings of morning on the docks. As the buildings catch the earliest announcements of the tropical sun, I turn west to watch that side of the dawn and notice I am no longer alone. Along a low, blue-and-white-tiled bench, a dozen men have assembled as if by command. As I watch sidelong, they peel oranges and sip from white Styrofoam cups, each man lean and a little bit tough-looking in the nonchalant street clothes of resort cowboys. They do not look like mariners, though I know they are bound to the ocean by seafaring ancestors.

On the perfect crescent beach in downtown Mazatlán, in fact, is an icon to fishing and the sea, to the primitive wealth of food from the vast unknown and the new wealth delivered in the form of tourists for whom the sea provides sport. I had passed the monument earlier and sketched it in my mind.

Forty feet high, the grandiose tribute to fishermen is executed in tile and white plaster. The central column is a lighthouse; from its base a giant serpentine arm spirals, wrapping a turn and a half around. Against those structures are the giant nude figures of a man and woman; he has a net and she reclines on the arm with one enormous foot on a billfish emerging from the base. In the head of the white-plaster fish is a startling blue-tile eye. Behind the woman are the figures of a shark and a porpoise entwined with one of her legs. All of this is set in a tile basin that apparently was a fountain at some time, but now is a stagnant pool of brown-green water.

At the docks, the boatmen talk in low rhythmic tones; it could be poetry. I pick out a few words, though, and hear instead the trivia of the morning, the bus ride to the docks, women, the lottery, how many of them will fish today. Not until all the customers show up will they know the answer to the last question. Soon, some of the men stand and walk to skiffs that they then row out to the cruisers anchored offshore; over the calm of the ending night is laid the grumbling of diesels, a sound I associate with the promise of a new fishing day.

Then I notice the blue glare from the fleet office behind the bench; inside a big, older man putters over a desk. I wander up the slight incline from the water, past the men left on the bench who barely acknowledge me. Guiding, after all, is really just selling local knowledge, which always supposes that the outsiders are beneath the insiders. I walk past a collection of tables and chairs on a covered patio—a kind of outdoor waiting room, obviously—and stand in the doorway of the office. The room is small, about twelve feet by twelve feet, furnished with a couple of couches, a desk and chair, and a coffee table piled with fishing magazines.

The walls are papered with thousands of photographs of fish and people, most of them in the common pose: A marlin, a sailfish, or a catch of tuna or dorado hang from a scaffold, with the anglers standing by. In one photo that grabs my eyes, a laughing woman is standing at the spar with her tackle, but instead of a fish it is a man strung up by his ankles. He, too, is laughing, upside-down. The walls also hold mounted fish—a striped marlin, a tiny swordfish, a sailfish, and a dorado whose wild colors under the fluorescent light are not easy on morning eyes.

The old man in the waiting room nods to me and asks, in English, "You fishing today?" I tell him I made my arrangements the evening before with another man who said I could fish for forty dollars American. He nods, asks my name, and jots it down on a scrap of paper on the desk. "You can fish with a young couple. They're coming soon, I think." And then he disappears into a back room, leaving me among the stories on the walls.

This scene is played here and in many similar offices on the harbor at Mazatlán and in the other ports on the Mexican Pacific at dawn every day, except when the rare gale or hurricane shuts down the fleets. Mazatlán, Guaymas, and the resorts of Baja California across the Sea of Cortez brought big game fishing to the American masses; another writer called it "democratizing" the sport. Organized charter fishing in Mexico is only a generation old, which not only means that the original characters are still around, but that the fishing is still quite good. The older, more heavily fished grounds of the Atlantic, Gulf, and California coasts have been worked over pretty hard because of their proximity to urban centers, but until long-range air travel became commonplace, the Mexican mainland and Baja peninsula ports were virtually isolated.

Fishing and everything else in Mexico is relatively inexpensive, making the cost of catching a billfish a bargain. You do lose the ambience of, say, Bimini or Cuba or Walker's Cay, but you aren't paying six hundred to a thousand dollars a day, either. (On the Mexican Pacific, you can find the high-bucks resorts at Cabo San Lucas, too, and the subdued elegance of some of the pioneer fish camps on the eastern Baja where big game resorts began in Mexico just thirty-five years ago.)

At about half past six, the muted sounds of the boatmen making ready are replaced by taxicabs and clattering moto-carts delivering the day's customers to the docks. From a pair of cabs emerge five men, all wearing straw hats with blue or red bandannas, who proceed to unload several coolers, cases of beer, and fishing gear. They call the man in the office by name, demonstrating familiarity and that this is a return trip. They ask if the boat they want is available, and the man in the office says it is and that they will leave when the bait and ice arrive.

The men, who make much of their obvious hangovers, collapse in the chairs on the patio, and fall to talking of the marlin and sailfish they are sure they will catch that day. One drinks a beer. The boatmen take care to avoid the patio, tending instead to the ice, which is soon dropped in blocks from a truck onto the dusty roadway. The bait—mullet—arrives in plastic bags with a man who is obviously a senior captain, judging from the deference of the others.

Two more parties of roughly the same dimensions as the first have joined the cast on the patio by the time my companions for the day arrive, hurrying from their cab, afraid they will miss the boat since they are a bit late. They are perhaps twenty or twenty-two, both blond and tanned, of average build; they look sleepy. He is wearing a straw cowboy hat; she has no hat at all until, while the man negotiates the charter, she buys one—a floppy straw hat—from a vendor who has materialized on the docks. He wears a stack of maybe twenty straw hats on his head and carries the women's version. Everywhere in Mazatlán, at every hour of the day and night, someone is trying to sell you something—hats, blankets, jewelry, condomin-

iums, fishing trips, statues of marlin. This is a tedious matter, unless you understand that tourists are more than just a sideline here in coastal Mexico; they are survival.

After she buys her hat, the woman takes a chair with the men on the patio and goes to sleep. Five minutes later, her companion comes from the office with the old man who begins dispatching the four boats that will fish today. He carefully sends the earliest arrivals out first, and they head for their boat, chattering, excited, like a bowling team that has made the finals. Some of the boatmen on the tile bench leave, not needed this morning.

The young man wakes the woman with a gentle shoulder rub, and as we wait for our boat, we introduce ourselves. Mike and Terri were married a week ago, missed their plane the day after their wedding because the party went on and on, but caught the next one. They have never been billfishing but decided to come to Mazatlán for their honeymoon, in part, because they saw a television program about big fish off Australia.

They are from New Mexico, where he is a carpenter and she is a clerk in an auto parts store. Their gold rings flash in the new light of the morning, and they cannot seem to be more than a couple of feet from each other. I tell them I am from Seattle, in Mazatlán just for the fishing. "Do you get seasick?" Terri asks me. "I'm a little worried about getting seasick," she says. Her husband ribs her about one too many tequilas the night before as we walk to the boat.

The old man says nothing as he leads us to our boat lying stern to the dock, idling. He seems grouchy, but I read into him a resignation at having dispatched thousands of boats and anglers, at having heard the same questions over and over, the main one being "How's the fishing going to be today?" which trickles from Mike as we board. "Perfect," the old man tells him and quick as that, the mate has let go the lines, and we are slipping ahead of our burbling wake and out of the teardrop harbor.

The boat is Spartan, to say the least, fiberglass, about forty-two feet, with a fair-size working deck on which three lawn chairs with heavy metal bases and rod sockets are placed, apparently the fighting chairs. Forward are a raised and covered middeck with Naugahyde settees port and starboard, with a companionway amidship leading to a barely finished cabin. Below are four plywood berths, sans mattresses, a workbench with a half-dozen door-knocker lures and some bait rigs, and an enclosed head. She seems seaworthy, I conclude, but with no frills.

As we round the jetty marker, I climb to the flying bridge and note that the boat has absolutely no electronic gear, no radar, fish-finders, loran, depth sounders — none of the technology that usually appears in pairs on offshore boats. Under the captain's bench on the port side, I see what looks like a tired CB radio in a Styrofoam cooler. The steering station on the port side is fronted by a magnetic compass, and that's it.

At the helm is a man in his sixties, dressed in slacks and a polo shirt, wearing a baseball hat with the emblem of a Montana truck stop. He is short, sun-dark, and taciturn. Neither he nor the mate has said a single word to us, and he only marginally acknowledges my presence on his bridge. I ask his name and he says, "Lopez." I ask him the mate's name. "Hector." End of conversation.

I watch Mazatlán recede into the haze. After awhile, I try Captain Lopez (no relation to Monty or Barry) again with my survival Spanish, eventually learning that his engine is a GM 671 diesel, that he has been a captain for twenty years, that his biggest fish was a 609-pound blue marlin "many years ago," and that the marlin are rarely over 300 pounds any more. He kills everything — no catch, tag, and release here — and gives the fish to "the

orphans" because Japanese commercial longliners, he says, will catch and kill them if he does not. He tells me there are far fewer fish now than just five years ago, and he shrugs his shoulders. He navigates by dead reckoning, using only compass and clock for the two-hour run.

The sea is flat calm, like a lake, but on deck, Terri is at the rail in the miserable clutches of *mal de mer* and no doubt contemplating a very long day. Mike helps Terri. Hector silently sews baits. I decide to stay with Captain Lopez on the flying bridge until we set the gear. The rods and reels are fairly lightweight, seven-foot rods with Penns of early vintage and ragged 80-pound test line. I see by Hector's preparations that we will fish baits from the riggers, which are just whisker poles from the cabin side, and lures from the flat lines.

Terri is through at the rail and trying to sleep on the settee, so I climb down to the deck and leave captain and mate to their doughnuts and sodas. "So Mike," I say, "how about if we take half-hours in the chair." He says fine. We talk, and I learn that he didn't know, for one thing, that we would be trolling constantly, that we would not stop and drop lines over the side like the headboats on which he had fished off California.

Mike knows enough about fishing to invoke magic, though. He has his hat, which he now calls his lucky hat, and he has an Arizona Indian chant that he begins as soon as Hector sets the gear. We are about twenty miles offshore to the northwest of Mazatlán, I estimate, in the jaws formed by the tip of Baja and the mainland. There, the central trench of the Sea of Cortez runs onto the relative shallows of the continental shelf. The flats are broken by deep canyons on the charts I have seen (none are in evidence aboard the boat) and the coastal upwelling over it all is one of the Pacific's great lunch lines.

At eleven o'clock, after two hours' trolling at about

three knots under a sizzling sun through absolutely undistinguished water — no rips, no birds, no nothing — Terri is in the chair, looking very pale but game; Mike is doing his fish chant behind her; Lopez and Hector are sequestered on the flying bridge; and I just happen to be watching when a sailfish hits the mullet on the left rigger. As Hector scrambles down the ladder, the sailfish gets airborne and the reel screams. The light through the fish's fanned dorsal is a supernatural blue, and the droplets of water shaking from its body fall like diamonds in the sun.

Hector tries to hand Terri the rod, and there ensues a tender moment in which she tries to talk her husband into taking the fish for himself. She insists, then he insists, and finally Hector gets fed up with the indecision and thrusts the rod at Terri, who never left the chair anyway. From the beginning, the sporting ethic of the International Game Fish Association is abandoned because clearly two people are fighting this fish. Hector helps Terri pump the sailfish up after it sounds, and eventually, Mike takes over from Hector.

Fighting the sailfish, Terri and Mike are transformed, initiated, and their excitement gives way to a cool, steady, instinctive brand of mutual encouragement. Mike loses his lucky hat over the side. Terri is no longer seasick. Mike keeps saying, "You got it, you got it. It's all yours," and I have the sense he is talking like a football coach from his not-too-distant past. Finally, Hector wires the good-size fish that will weigh out later at 110 pounds, and as he raises his club, Terri howls, "Don't kill it." Hector ignores her, kills the fish, and brings it aboard.

Mike comforts Terri, who is clearly tired and now upset. He takes her hand and brings her to the stern, to the sailfish, still bronze and silver and cobalt blue. He doesn't know so he can't tell her that this amazing animal began its life as one of maybe 4 million eggs squeezed into the sea by its mother-fish, that it has survived as prey and predator for five or six years to reach this size. Sailfish are plentiful, and swim in the midlatitudes of every ocean; they are often the first billfish caught by a big game angler. The world record on the Pacific is 221 pounds; on the Atlantic, 128 pounds.

"Touch it," Mike says, reaching down to explore the dorsal slit in the back of the fish. Terri touches the sailfish, tentatively at first, and then more boldly. She runs her hand along the bright blue dorsal fin, then the bill, and then under the fish's mouth where the skin is dark and leathery, not at all fishlike. "Its eyes are the same color as Paul Newman's," she says to Mike. Hector ignores the scene on deck, no doubt he has witnessed it before, and tends to the gear. Terri pats the fish gently on the side of its head. "Poor baby," she says. "Poor baby."

The combination of prime fishing water and luxury ashore at Golfito Sailfish Rancho made it one of the premier hot spots in the late 1980s. The trade magazines were full of stories about the development of first-class accommodations and lots of fish, particularly sailfish. In January 1990, for instance, over a thousand billfish were raised, half of them hooked, and about three hundred boated or released. All but one of those caught were sailfish. Dorado, roosterfish, and that occasional blue marlin round out the fast action.

The aboriginal inhabitants of this narrow verdant land in Central America have been connected to the sea for eons, tending traps, nets, and lines for the abundant food just off the pristine beaches. Now, visiting anglers hunt big game fish in open skiffs with sun tarps known as pangas.

The acrobatic, neon air show of the dorado, which often hits the baits in large schools to provide plenty of action, particularly on light tackle. An added attraction follows at dinner, since most resort kitchens will cook your catch and the dorado is a true crowd pleaser.

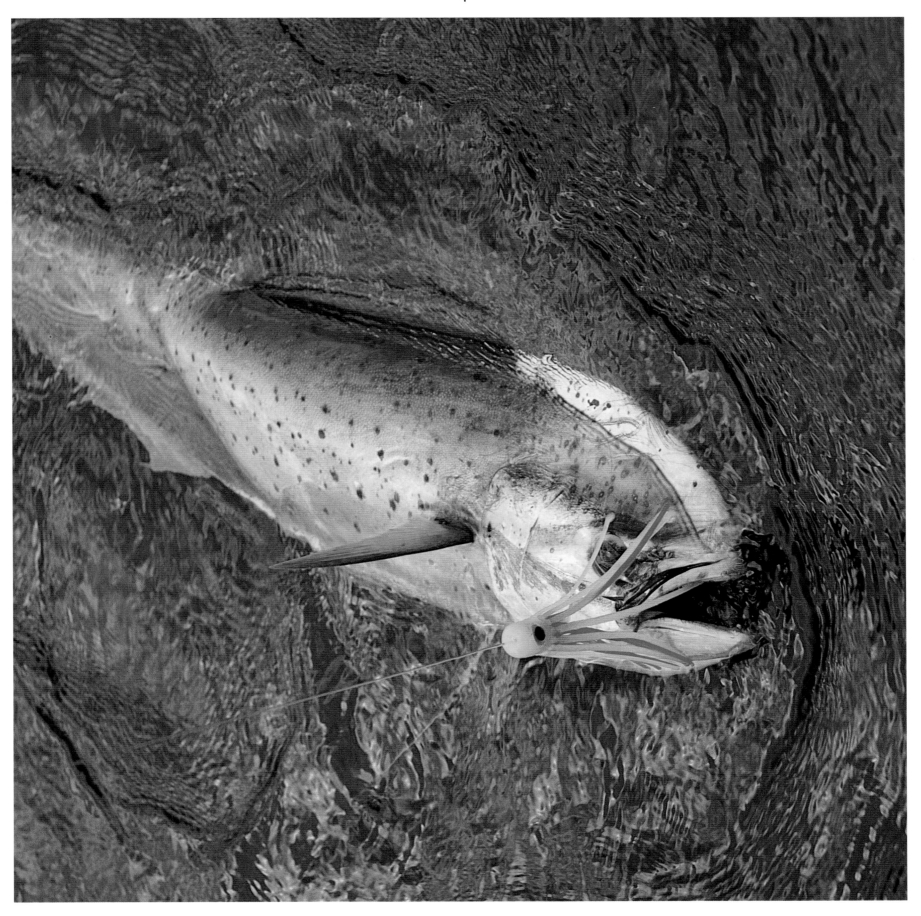

The sailfish's bronze color is only one of many hues in the palette of dancing skin tones of all billfish, produced by a unique layer of cells that respond to fear, anger, and other impulses. This fish was taken by Mike Labarbra off Costa Rica. There's an extra bonus to fishing in Costa Rica, the colors provided by Mother Nature.

Dawn off Central America delivers yet another reason to get up and go fishing.

KEEPING SCORE

The virtue of the hare is not in having it but in the pursuit of it. — Pascal

We were blind-casting for tarpon in midafternoon on the glassy harbor at Isla Mujeres, talking about running offshore later for sailfish, when the tournament boats started to arrive. I had a fish on, in fact, about 50 pounds of powerful, chrome muscle holding firm about two hundred yards from our panga after an air show and nonstop run that took my light spinning reel down to the spool. I was fishing with a man I'll call Pearl, a black-market guide of the sort you'll find in many ports who will take you fishing under clandestine circumstances for very little money.

Pearl is an expatriated American whose life, once revealed, includes a couple of years in a famous Florida bar band followed by some dark commerce, semilegal trading in goods from mahogany to T-shirts. His intentions, he said, have always been clear to him, though. "Life is not a test. I am going to enjoy myself." When I met him, through mutual friends, his current incarnation was a blend of Gauguin and Kip Farrington, painting and fishing on a small island off the Yucatán Peninsula, just getting by but looking very relaxed. "I love fishing. I go fishing nearly every day, in my own boat," he said. "If I can pick up a little money and some good company, that's fine. If not, that's fine too."

His girlfriend—also an American I'll call Molly, though that isn't her real name either—was beautiful, friendly, and at ease in the panga, which she often ran expertly when we were chasing a fish. She opened beer pop tabs with long, lavender-painted fingernails that seemed none the worse for wear and took an occasional photograph with her yellow waterproof camera.

All official sport fishing on Isla Mujeres is controlled by a syndicate of elders and entrepreneurs who do not take kindly to free-lancers. We'd started the day at ten o'clock from a beach north of town where the departure of a very pale tourist and a tanned couple with fishing gear would go relatively unnoticed. Sailfish, maybe blue marlin, were in the plan as well (for the meager fee), but tarpon after tarpon—virtually every cast along this particular underwater shelf—was hard to leave. They hit everything we threw at them, feathered poppers that look like bass plugs in Halloween costumes, Rapalas, and an odd, bent-metal darting lure in bright pink.

Pearl knew just where to be, and we made long drifts along the shelf under the hot sun. The 95°F April heat and sopping humidity seemed to draw moisture from the sea to coat our bodies; we were dripping wet. This was wonderful fishing, though, made more so by the open boat, light tackle, and low budget. And even with a fish on, Pearl kept up a running patter in his languid drawl, telling me stories about what he called his "addiction" to the Caribbean, in whose northwesternmost reaches we were fishing at Isla Mujeres.

He talked about the extremes of this zone between 10 and 20 degrees north, just above the equator, about the insane gales, the hurricanes, and the balm of warmth and kindly breezes. He told me he knew pirates, renegades of every national stripe who seized boats and put the owners in their dinghies to drift and die. He said he had seen free-jumping giant blue marlin he estimated to be over 1,000 pounds; and once, when he was down on his luck, he'd lived well for months alone on a beach foraging on a reef near shore. He said he was in Isla "for business reasons" but would soon sell his panga and go to Venezuela. "Bill-fishing is getting to be a religion down there," he said. "They outlawed everything but sport fishing off part of

their coast." That was in the early 1980s.

Pearl told me about his life "under the shrimp," which was his way of describing the shape of the archipelago that runs along the eastern edge of the Caribbean. From Cuba (the head), the shrimp follows the Greater Antilles eastward, curves around at Puerto Rico and down to the south along the Leeward and Windward groups in a tightening gyre speckled with islands whose names alone evoke exotic imagery: the Virgins, Antigua and Barbuda, Martinique, Barbados, Grenada. Then the shrimp illusion on a chart dissolves in the coastal islands of Venezuela, colonial remnants like Aruba, Curacao, Bonaire. The Caribbean's western encounter with the earth's junior partner—dry land—comes on the Central American coast where the terrain breaks from lush jungles onto astonishing beaches and reefs, countries whose names now evoke the sadnesses of festering greed and tangled politics—Panama, Costa Rica, Nicaragua, Honduras, Guatemala—and then back to the hook of the Yucatán Peninsula.

The sea floor to which the islands, reefs, and coastlines are attached is a wrinkled basin with a mix of canyons and ridges that urge rich upwellings of nutrients. The currents and tidal disturbances keep the zooplankton and phytoplankton in circulation to feed the invertebrates (for the most part) that in turn feed the vertebrates.

"I've had a good life here, by accident," Pearl tells me, changing lures with practiced efficiency, barely glancing at his hands. He looks to be approaching forty at the moment. "I started out in Mobile, dirt poor, and this place took care of me."

I take a break, so Molly picks up a rod and almost immediately is working on a big tarpon that runs a couple hundred yards of line off at about sixty miles per hour, swimming just under the surface to make a hump in the water. "God, I love that," Pearl says about the tarpon's fierce, steady run. He and I have bet dinner on the largest fish, agreeing that Molly and consensus would decide the winner, rather than the precision of weighing since we were releasing everything. She didn't want to bet but said she would consider eating with us later, especially if the beach huts were full of the tournament crews. It is a rare fishing day that doesn't include a similar contest, no matter what you're catching.

"I spent a lot of time hitchhiking around as a mate on tournament boats like the ones over there," Pearl says, pointing to what has become a parade of sport-fishing yachts entering the harbor. "These guys are probably going to Cozumel, down the coast about eighty miles. Their big tournament is coming up pretty quick. The owners who do the actual fishing usually fly down because they're busy making the kind of money it takes to own one. The skippers and mates take care of the boats. Sometimes they charter them when the owner isn't around; sometimes they just hang out. You can get enough experience to be a mate in a couple of months if you're young and strong and a little bit smart," he says, beginning a loose ramble about tournaments that I will later punctuate with reading and other conversations.

The boats are jockeying around at the entrance to the single marina at Isla, sorting out the dock space, graceful even with their ungainly aluminum tuna towers and outriggers. The great offshore fishing yachts—Rybovich, Bertram, Hatteras, Carolina, Merritt, Buddy Davis, Sportsman, Ocean, Striker, Kincheloe-Nickerson (to name a few)—are near the pinnacle of human adventure on the sea. These international travelers ranging in size from forty to seventy feet are powered by twin turbo diesel or gas engines at speeds of thirty knots or better, with luxurious, air-conditioned compartments for owner and crew. Figure $350,000 to maybe $2 million just to buy one. Hitting the big-time international tournament circuit, though, is an entirely different matter than just owning a boat and going fishing once in awhile.

Big game tournament fishing is so compelling, so seductive, it even has its own four-color, glossy magazine—*Tournament Digest*—that reports every other month on the results of the hundreds of marlin, swordfish, sailfish, tuna, shark, and other events each year. All the sportfishing magazines cover the tournaments, and one—*Marlin*—once offered readers a print-out of the year's tournaments for five dollars. The list on computer paper, which the editors tell you is not by any means complete, is an inch thick and names four hundred saltwater tournaments held off North America and around the world. Double that number is probably closer to the truth.

The term *tournament* generally describes fishing in competition with other anglers, but as with any other game, the varieties are just about unlimited. Most common among big game tournaments are the local affairs, sponsored by just about every one of the hundreds of angling clubs, in which members and guests hit the local waters, make side bets, and award trophies to each other. These usually include a few days' fishing and a big party. Then there are long-running tournaments, like the Metropolitan South Florida Fishing Tournament, in which the entrants pay a fee and fish for months. The Met has been run from December to May for over fifty years by the *Miami Herald* newspaper; it covers thirty-six species (including big game fish), line classes, areas, and age divisions. As far as I know, it's the biggest fishing tournament in the world, with thousands of anglers participating and an ambience rivaling that of a state fair.

About 10 to 20 percent of big game tournaments have heavy commercial sponsorship, either by gear or boat manufacturers, and some require entrants to own a particular kind of boat. The annual Bertram–Hatteras "Shoot Out" in the Bahamas is an example of that variety. And almost all resorts and fishing ports have their annual tournaments, some for local charities like the famous "Boy Scout" tournament, a.k.a. the Virgin Islands Open. Many tournaments are part of a series, like the Bahamas championship, in which anglers campaign in several tournaments for an entire season in one region.

The cash prizes in these tournaments run into the hundreds of thousands of dollars, and a few anglers, skippers, and boats actually approach the events with profit in mind. Side bets, or calcuttas as they are called, are made for very large amounts of money, often in seven or even eight figures.

Generally, tournaments can be classed as either *kill* or *release* contests. In the former, fish over a certain weight limit are killed and landed, although points are often awarded for released fish even in kill tournaments. In the latter, all billfish are released; observers verify the catches, and the data on the tags planted in the fish are sent to fisheries biologists managing the area. Some clubs prohibit members from participating in kill tournaments in support of conservation of the fish, and generally, the inverted flags signifying released billfish fly more frequently from the halyards of returning tournament boats.

In the 1980s, a series of international tournaments caught on in which anglers qualify for teams and compete for their home countries or regions. "A lot of people like the team tournaments," Richard Gibson, the managing editor of *Tournament Digest*, told me. "If you take away the dollars and fish for pride and trophies, the feelings around the tournaments are entirely different, much more fun. A lot of people don't really know how much money is involved in some of these tournaments, how much pressure there is to produce."

Because the action in fishing tournaments takes place offshore, they don't draw crowds like the Super Bowl, and you have to be an aficionado to even keep track of who's who. "People seem to be by nature competitive," Gibson says. "They are going to go fishing anyway, and if they fish in a tournament, somebody can walk away with a couple of hundred thousand dollars. The attraction is limited to people who can afford it, though. Big game tournament fishing is the number one participant sport among active millionaires, and I think a lot of them get into tournament fishing for reasons of vanity. Everybody likes to win something."

The biggest tournament of all is the International Game Fish Association record book, which has run for fifty years. The 1989 edition contains 3,113 world fishing records in a 240-page volume, listing the biggest freshwater and saltwater fish ever caught by species and breaking strength of the line, in men's and women's divisions, with fly-fishing records listed separately. The book also has descriptions of the species, illustrations of each, and other information relating to conservation and management. You get a copy of the record book when you join the IGFA for as little as thirty dollars (contributing member); getting your name in the book could cost you thousands, even millions.

Ernest Hemingway said that the only important records were "firsts," because then nobody could take them away from you. Since 1939, the IGFA has kept records to be broken, set the rules for anglers based on conservation ethics inaugurated by the Catalina Tuna Club in 1898, and awarded no prizes. In 1983, the IGFA started its 5:1, 10:1, 15:1, and 20:1 clubs, which are lists of anglers who catch fish whose weights exceed the breaking strength of the line by those proportions.

Becoming listed as a world record holder has been a

matter of pure luck or single-minded pursuit over the years. In 1943, for instance, a young airman named Baxter Ross set the world all-tackle record for mako shark off New Zealand on his first and only fishing trip, landing a 1,000-pound monster. (The current record for mako was set at 1,115 pounds by Patrick Guillanton, off Mauritius, on November 16, 1988.) As long as an angler has followed the two pages of rules, which really are straightforward, and has witnesses to the catch, the IGFA will award the record from its Fort Lauderdale office.

The occasional stroke of beginner's luck, though, is the exception rather than the rule in the IGFA record book, and in the case of big game fish, dogged pursuit is more common. Some anglers, most notably, Jerry Dunaway and Deborah Maddux (see "Frank, Three, and Monty: The Business of Big Fish") in recent years, spend virtually all their time and literally millions of dollars in pursuit of the various line class records for big fish.

At first glance, the lighter line class records for marlin, sailfish, and the other big game species are almost too astounding to be believed. Consider Deborah Maddux's Atlantic sailfish record of 72 pounds 12 ounces on 2-pound test line, set off Senegal in 1988. (Two-pound test monofilament line is barely stronger than ordinary sewing thread.) Or Jerry Dunaway's 231-pound 9-ounce Atlantic blue marlin taken on 8-pound test line off the Ivory Coast the same year. (The Atlantic blue marlin record on 2-pound test line is vacant as of 1989.) Setting a record for a big fish on light line isn't terribly sporting in some cases, though the rules are always technically followed. Often the fish is brought to the wire (or heavy leader that can be fifteen feet long in classes up to 20 pounds) by very skillful use of the boat, backing down on a hooked fish with very little pressure, if any, brought by the rod.

"This is my kind of fishing, though," says Pearl, finishing his reminiscence on tournaments. We are drifting with the motor off, listening to the birds, and Molly hands him a beer, her fingernails flashing in the lowering sun. "I never did care for the pressure. You can get pretty worked up about the money and winning, but it's just a way of keeping score. I like it quiet, like now."

We were done with the tarpon for the day, sliding out of the harbor for an evening across the reef with the sailfish. "We'll catch up with those guys later. I probably know some of them," Pearl says, waving as we pass the docks. "Hey. Remember I told you about seeing marlin jumping by themselves. One time was right out there, right past that point where we're going."

The society of big game anglers takes some of its flavor from the rituals and chores of dock-side life. "Catch anything?" is an opening line of a quick conversation while you button up the boat for the night, or the beginning of a long story possibly to be continued at a nearby watering hole.

A single trip to a tackle shop in a fishing port lets you know that
rods and reels are more than just tools, and the places you buy them
are more than pure commerce. Just about everybody has a favorite, a home tackle
dealer, and harbors tend to bring out the same kinds of loyalties.

Pioneer tackle builder Mickey Altenkirch on the dock on Long Island, New York, with one of his creations. A substantial subculture of tackle addicts has grown up since the turn of the century when we approached the challenge of taking fish like half-ton mako shark with rod and reel. Some fine collections are found in fishing ports; most are private but some are on display in local museums. All reveal a hunter's instinct for combining the strength and efficiency that will suddenly be summoned in full when a big fish strikes.

Hemingway's memorabilia, displayed in The Compleat Angler *on Bimini, reveal the enormous energy the author brought to fishing. He, Zane Grey, Kip Farrington, Alfred Glassell, Jr., and Michael Lerner (to name but a few) are senior members of a society of anglers you can join any time.*

Artist John Doyle's vision of a giant blue marlin, alone at sea, feeding on yellowfin tuna. He calls it Cha-cha-cha.

A
BLUEWATER
PRIMER

Only the most extraordinary powers of adaptation, both in bodily form and habit, have made it possible for the fishes to become the most successful class of all the backboned animals and to achieve the mastery of the waters. — Joy O. I. Spoczynska, *An Age of Fishes*

Imagine this: Dawn has come. Its brightening promise on the horizon flirts with towering cumulus clouds to cast long shadows on a sea made wild by a rising gale. The ocean's surface is shredded by enormous waves that would frighten a mariner, though at this moment no human eyes survey the scene. No ships or boats are near, no jet contrails are overhead, no witnesses are present (which, of course, is why imagination is necessary).

The sounds of the roaring wind and the fierce crack of water splitting from water heighten suddenly, announcing a wave much larger than its cousins. The rogue, forty feet from trough to crest, passes across the plane of the imaginary moment. In its thundering mass, we see silhouetted hundreds of chrome shapes, apparently a school of big fish of some kind. In the slick of the suction at the base of the watery edifice, the sea boils with the fish as they race ahead of the wave.

Then, as though on the command of some divine choreographer, the fish take to the air at once, obviously driven from their comfortable ocean by some unspeakable terror. They are yellowfin tuna, astounding packages of muscle trimmed with bright finlets that give their backs a saw-blade appearance. Behind them, an apparition materializes that tests the imagination: A giant blue marlin, arched and flashing purple and silver and red, explodes from the face of the wave, its black bill carving the air as it pursues the tuna.

The marlin — a female — weighs a ton and a half, one of the great specimens we only suppose are out there because we know the true monsters are never seen. She is traveling, feeding constantly, and she has hurtled up from the

OCEAN ECOLOGY

depths through the school of yellowfin to stun and weaken some of them. Now, she distends the leathery skin beneath her bill root to reveal a toothless cavern that in an instant envelops her prey. The tuna, a big fish of perhaps 300 pounds, disappears into the great marlin's gullet, and she returns to the sea behind the passing wave.

Such a drama of the oceanic food web is played unseen all the time, more often than we dry-land humans drive to work or lie down to sleep or even feed ourselves. It is hard to come to terms with such mystery, or to understand that likely our fate is to never know the sea. One marine biologist I know is fond of saying that we know less about the oceans than we do about the moon. Though he is given to hyperbole, the exaggeration is not far off. Without a doubt, the seduction of big game angling has much to do with involving ourselves in the ocean's mysteries. Encounters with the great fish and their environment are as thrilling for most of us as a trip to the moon.

Fish have demonstrated a remarkable ability to adapt to the ecosystem of planet Earth, or more accurately, planet Ocean, since water forms seven-eighths of everything we know. Over 90 percent of all vertebrates are fish, the most successful class of creatures, and they have thrived and evolved in every body of water on earth. As Joy Spoczynska points out in her excellent book, *An Age of Fishes*, the fishes, of all classes of creatures, are most synchronized with the planet's rhythms. Since most living things are more water than not, it is advan-

tageous for a creature to live in an environment such as the sea in which it does not need to expend so much energy to conserve and produce water.

This harmony with water, the nature of water itself, and the characteristics of water existing in great quantities like the oceans offer a framework onto which we can graft bits of knowledge. We do have some idea of how the marine ecosystem works and how animals have adapted to life on the ocean planet (partly because of data gathering by sport anglers). The governing generalities of the marine environment are a product of nutrients, light, and circulation.

First, every living creature is both predator and prey, consumer and food. The forms that make up the marine food web have adapted to span levels of complexity from single-celled organisms to the intricate systems of the blue marlin that include heating tissue, a brain, and a sophisticated digestive tract. Hence, marlin can and do eat just about anything that swims.

Many species participate in the nourishment cycle in different ways at various levels of their development from egg to adult. For example, of the billions of blue marlin eggs squeezed into the sea during a spawning season, most will become prey. But a few will grow to become apex predators, prey for very few other animals.

The more complex an organism, the more difficult it is to replace it. Phytoplankton, the microscopic plants that form a big part of the marine nutrient web, can double in number in a day. Replacing a dead mature marlin, however, requires good genes, years, and much good luck.

The predator–prey dance that accounts so profoundly for adaptation (survival of the fittest) is performed in the saline soup of the sea, and therefore the condition of the sea itself is critical. Only certain things can happen in cold water, other things in warm, and so forth through various conditions of temperature and salinity and various levels of light. Circulation of water and its nutrient packages can be vertical, as in daily heat- or light-stimulated movement, and horizontal, as in ocean currents and upwellings over subsurface terrain.

The colder the water, the more vertical circulation occurs. The water on the surface is coldest; surface mixing, air temperature, and just being heavier makes cold water sink, producing vertical mixing as warmer water from below rises to replace it. In the midlatitude seas (say Canada to Costa Rica), such mixing is seasonal; in the warm seas (say Costa Rica to Peru), very little vertical mixing occurs, concentrating the nutrients and oxygen in the upper layers of the sea. (This is one reason that certain regions offer better fishing at some times of the year than others.)

Most photosynthesis that produces the microscopic nourishment in the outer tiers of the marine food web occurs in the sea's top three hundred feet where light can penetrate. Without circulation—both horizontal and vertical—the ocean below that top layer would be virtually inert except for the sinking organic matter that is pulled by gravity to the bottom. Nothing like the multiple layers of the earth's fertile seas would exist without circulation.

Though humans are conversant with the broad concepts of the oceans, the natural systems of selection and survival depend on endless complex variables. Hence, we have the abiding sense—or should have—that human incursion into the marine habitat as a predator can produce unexpected and potentially disastrous results.

Predators limit the populations of their prey directly, and vice versa. If, for instance, we (as predators) dramatically decrease the biomass of sardines off the Southern California coast, the larger fish that depend on the sardines will respond by dying off, reducing their size and ability to eat sardines over the span of a few generations, or going elsewhere in search of food. The smaller forms on which the absent

A sharp angler's eyes can pick out not only the sailfish getting flight time, but also others finning on the ocean's surface off Costa Rica.

sardines feed could also increase to numbers so great that they would in turn reduce the viability of their prey, perhaps the larval form of one of the sardines' predators, and on and on and on.

In reality, the disappearance of sardines off California was probably part of a natural cycle and part overfishing by commercial packers. The consequent reduction of marlin, swordfish, and tuna populations is only a small link in the complex chain.

Precisely because predator–prey relationships are so complicated and, from the human point of view, so unpredictable in their outcome, fisheries managers do not like to consider them in their formulas. But since we interact with marine animals for both food and pleasure, we are compelled to attempt to understand the effects of those interactions and to ease the negative consequences to the ecosystem.

The only thing we know for sure about our interaction with the great fish is that we don't know enough about them. Though we probably will never come to grips with the cosmic equations by which populations of sea creatures fluctuate, we can determine their ages, numbers, and habits. By increasing our understanding of the apex predators, we can infer conditions of the sea in the tiers of the food web beneath them. Almost certainly, the health of the great game fish of the offshore grounds is a barometer by which we can measure the health of the ocean planet.

To find and catch big game fish, find their food. To become a responsible ocean ecologist, support the International Game Fish Association, The Billfish Foundation, and other national and local organizations dedicated to learning more about the seas and their creatures.

Since 1898 when offshore fishing with rods and reels began off Santa Catalina Island, California, we have come to regard ten species as big game fish. Though such a relativistic consideration is arbitrary, for this book, and others that have preceded it, the big game fish are broadbill swordfish, black marlin, blue marlin, striped marlin, white marlin, sailfish, spearfish, bluefin tuna, yellowfin tuna, and mako shark.

Because angling is an uncertain proposition, fishermen hunting the big game species frequently and happily catch a variety of other fish in the course of their days at sea. We are, therefore, including references to dolphin, albacore, bigeye tuna, blackfin tuna, black skipjack, kawakawa, little tunny, king mackerel, skipjack, and wahoo.

Here are brief descriptions of the Big Ten Plus, along with the current world all-tackle records and record holders as certified by the International Game Fish Association:

THE BIG TEN . . .

Broadbill swordfish, *Xiphias gladius*: 1,182 pounds, by Lou Marron, off Iquique, Chili, May 7, 1953. The swordfish is in a family by itself, *Xiphiidae*, which means that no other organism on the planet has taken the same evolutionary route to survival. Known earlier as marlin swordfish, and later as broadbill or just swordfish, these exotic predators live in the warm and temperate seas around the globe. Adults have no scales, no teeth, and startling large blue eyes.

Black marlin, *Makaira indica*: 1,560 pounds, by Alfred Glassell, Jr., off Cabo Blanco, Peru, August 4, 1953. Black marlin are indigenous only to the Pacific and Indian oceans. They vary widely in appearance from dark blue to milky-white; the Japanese, in fact, call them *shirokajiki*, which means white marlin. Reliable claims of hooking and losing blacks in the 3,000-pound range make this magnificent animal the true giant of the fish

THE BIG TEN PLUS

kingdom. Like other marlins, the big fish are always female, with males reaching only a fifth of their size.

Blue marlin, *Makaira nigricans*: Pacific, 1,376 pounds by Jay Wm. deBeaubien, off Kona, Hawaii, May 31, 1982; Atlantic, 1,282 pounds by Larry Martin, off the Virgin Islands, August 6, 1977. A giant blue marlin was Santiago's noble adversary in *The Old Man and the Sea*, and the big game fish most familiar in anglers' dreams. Until recently, Atlantic and Pacific blue marlin were classed as separate species, primarily because of minor variations in size and coloration. Their range is worldwide in the temperate latitudes, extended northward or southward by the seasonal shifts in major currents like the Gulf Stream.

Striped marlin, *Tetrapturus audax*: 494 pounds by Bill Boniface, off Tutukaka, New Zealand, January 16, 1986. These smaller relatives of the true giants dwell in abundance in the midlatitudes of the Pacific and Indian oceans. With their cousins, the Atlantic whites, they are the most common marlins taken by sport anglers. Despite their familiarity, we know little about them, or any other marlins. Striped marlin seem to remain in local groups, rather than migrate in ocean-girdling currents, and so are a major target for Asian commercial longline fleets.

White marlin, *Tetrapturus albidus*: 181 pounds 14 ounces, by Evandro Luis Coser, off Vitória, Brazil, December 8, 1979. Confined to the Atlantic, this species is quite abundant. White marlin are the smallest of the four acknowledged types of marlins and are distinguished by their rounded fin tips; all other marlins have fins with pointed tips. Prized for acrobatics on light tackle, the white marlin have become the mainstay of big game angling from waters off New England to South America in the Western Hemisphere.

Sailfish, *Istiophorus platypterus*: Pacific, 221 pounds by C. W. Stewart, off Santa Cruz Island, Ecuador, February 12, 1947; Atlantic, 128 pounds 1 ounce by Harm Steyn, off Luanda, Angola, March 27, 1974. Records are kept separately for the Atlantic and Pacific groups of sailfish because of the extreme difference in average size. Other taxonomic considerations classed them as separate species until recently and included a third sailfish indigenous to the Indian Ocean. Sailfish of all groups are relatively abundant and are often the first billfish landed by a sport angler.

Shortbill spearfish, *Tetrapturus angustirostris*, and longbill spearfish, *T. pfluegeri*: 90 pounds 13 ounces by Joseph Larkin, off Madeira, near Portugal, June 2, 1980. Practically nothing is known about these uncommon big game fish save what is immediate in their appearance and where they are landed. The shortbill is native to the Pacific, the longbill to the Atlantic, and several local types including a Mediterranean spearfish occur as well. Prized by offshore anglers for their rarity, they are included in a single record class.

Bluefin tuna, *Thunnus thynnus*: 1,496 pounds by Ken Fraser, off Nova Scotia, Canada, October 26, 1979. In 1923, a Boston newspaper reported that a bluefin tuna weighing about 1,600 pounds was landed by a commercial fisherman. These beautiful, steel-gray and blue giants of the mackerel family are found worldwide in temperate and subtropical zones, appearing seasonally during fairly predictable migrations. More is known about tunas than about other big game fish because of their enormous food value. The first big game fish taken on rod and reel was a 183-pound bluefin tuna, off Catalina Island, California, on June 1, 1898.

Yellowfin tuna, *Thunnus albacares*: 388 pounds 12 ounces by Curt Weisenhutter, off San Benedicto Island, Mexico, April 1, 1977. Like the other tunas, the yellowfin are a member of the finlet group of fishes and among the most important food animals in the world. They are fast, with streamlined bodies, highly migratory, and abundant, occurring in enormous schools that often cover acres of the ocean's surface. Yellowfin are more numerous in the Pacific than in the Atlantic, ranging in both oceans in midlatitude 60–80°F water. Surprisingly, the yellowfin are warm-blooded. Some taxonomists separate the regional groups of yellowfin into separate species.

Mako shark, *Isurus oxyrhynchus*: 1,115 pounds by Patrick Guillanton, off Mauritius, November 16, 1988. The mako's spectacular and very unsharklike leaping ability and delicious taste make it a big game angler's prize. Although found in all oceans, makos migrate to find the seasonally warmer waters they prefer. Called the bonita shark by many, the Pacific version, although larger, is probably the same animal. The mako is one of the very few natural enemies of the swordfish.

PLUS . . .

Dolphin, *Coryphaena hippurus*: 87 pounds by Manuel Salazar, in the Papagayo Gulf, off Costa Rica, September 25, 1976. This prolific blue-water clown ranges abundantly in the temperate waters of all oceans. Favored by anglers for a great fight and a great meal, the dolphin— a.k.a. mahimahi and, less commonly, dorado—is a spectacular combination of dancing colors and voracious strikes.

Albacore, *Thunnus alalunga*: 88 pounds 2 ounces by Siegfried Dickemann, off Gran Canaria, Canary Islands, November 19, 1977. The albacore or longfin tuna are very popular with the charter fleets off California. The big West Coast run is from July to October, but albacore range in lesser schools in both the Pacific and Atlantic. Albacore are the "white-meat" tuna favored by canners.

Bigeye tuna, *Thunnus obesus*: Pacific, 435 pounds by Russel V. A. Lee, off Cabo Blanco, Peru, April 17, 1957; Atlantic, 375 pounds 8 ounces by Cecil Browne, off Ocean City, Maryland, August 26, 1977. Second largest of the tunas, though relatively uncommon to sport anglers, the bigeye are distinguished from yellowfin by subtle anatomical differences. Atlantic and Pacific variations were once thought to be separate species.

Blackfin tuna, *Thunnus atlanticus*: 42 pounds by Alan J. Card, off Bermuda, June 2, 1978. These small tuna range only in the western Atlantic, off the coast from Massachusetts to Brazil. They are delicious and often a bonus

Michael Leech, the director of the International Game Fish Association, at his office in Fort Lauderdale, Florida.

when they appear in large schools for spawning, from April to November, off Florida.

Black skipjack, *Euthynnus lineatus*: 20 pounds 5 ounces by Roger Torriero, off Baja California, Mexico, October 14, 1983. Of the three sport-caught members of the bonito family, the Pacific variation is the most common. The Pacific, or California, bonito ranges from British Columbia south to Baja, where its southern cousin takes over until Peru.

Kawakawa, *Euthynnus affinis*: 29 pounds by Ronald Nakamura, off Clarion Island, Mexico, December 17, 1986. These small tuna range in the warm waters of the Indian and Pacific oceans, with most sport catches reported off Mexico and the Hawaiian Islands.

Little tunny, *Euthynnus alletteratus*: 27 pounds by William E. Allison, off Key Largo, Florida, April 20, 1976. This small tuna and several close and hard-to-distinguish cousins are common in all oceans. The little tunny will only be familiar to anglers on the Atlantic.

King mackerel, *Scomberomorus cavalla*: 90 pounds by Norton I. Thomton, off Key West, Florida, February 16, 1976. Also called kingfish or cavalla, these fish are a target for many Atlantic coast anglers. King mackerel are the equivalent of the Pacific albacore as the staple for the headboat charter fleet.

Skipjack, *Euthynnus pelamis*: 41 pounds 14 ounces by Edmund K. R. Heinzen, off Mauritius, November 12, 1985. Found around the world in the warmest tropical zones, skipjack are usually caught in massive schools. Getting into them with light tackle is a rare treat.

Wahoo, *Acanthocybium solanderi*: 149 pounds by John Porovano, off Cat Cay, Bahamas, June 15, 1962. No disappointment to anglers trolling for marlin and other bigger fish, wahoo are a fight and a half under most conditions. They can be found around the world in warm waters. And they're tasty.

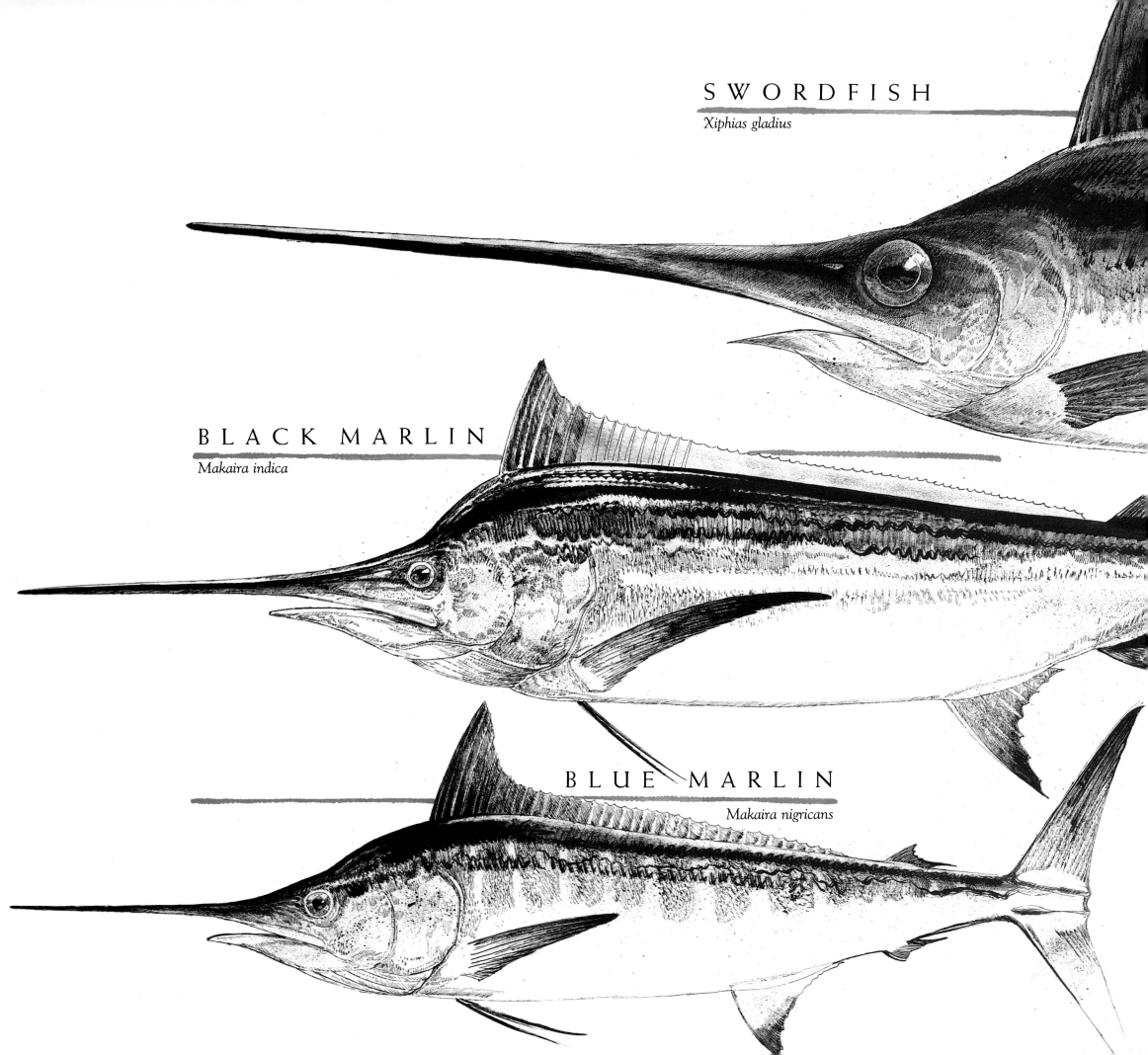

SWORDFISH
Xiphias gladius

BLACK MARLIN
Makaira indica

BLUE MARLIN
Makaira nigricans

STRIPED MARLIN
Tetrapturus audax

WHITE MARLIN
Tetrapturus albidus

MAKO SHARK
Isurus oxyrhynchus

SAIL FISH
Istiophorus platypterus

SHORTBILL SPEARFISH
Tetrapturus angustirostris

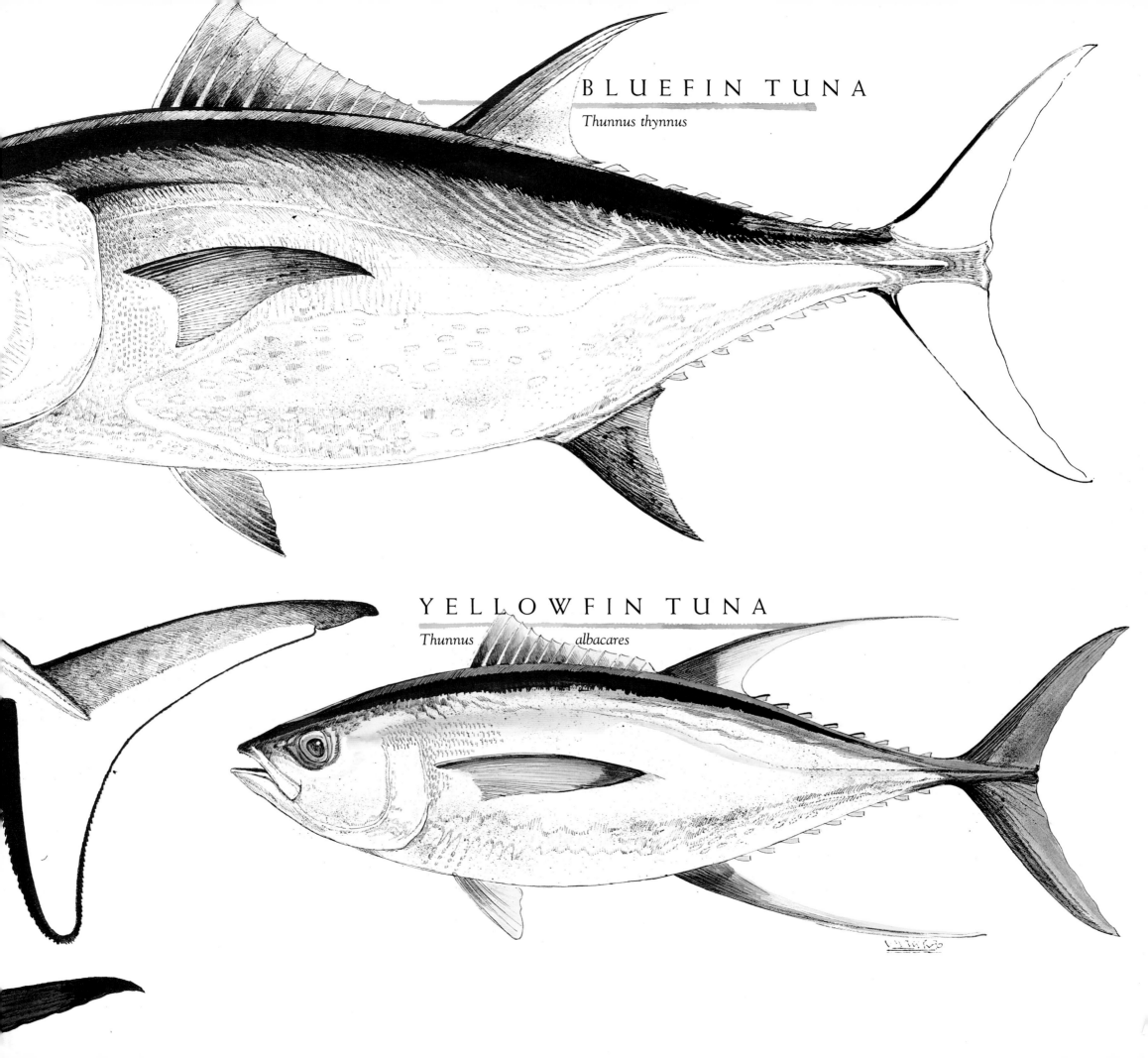

BLUEFIN TUNA

Thunnus thynnus

YELLOWFIN TUNA

Thunnus   albacares

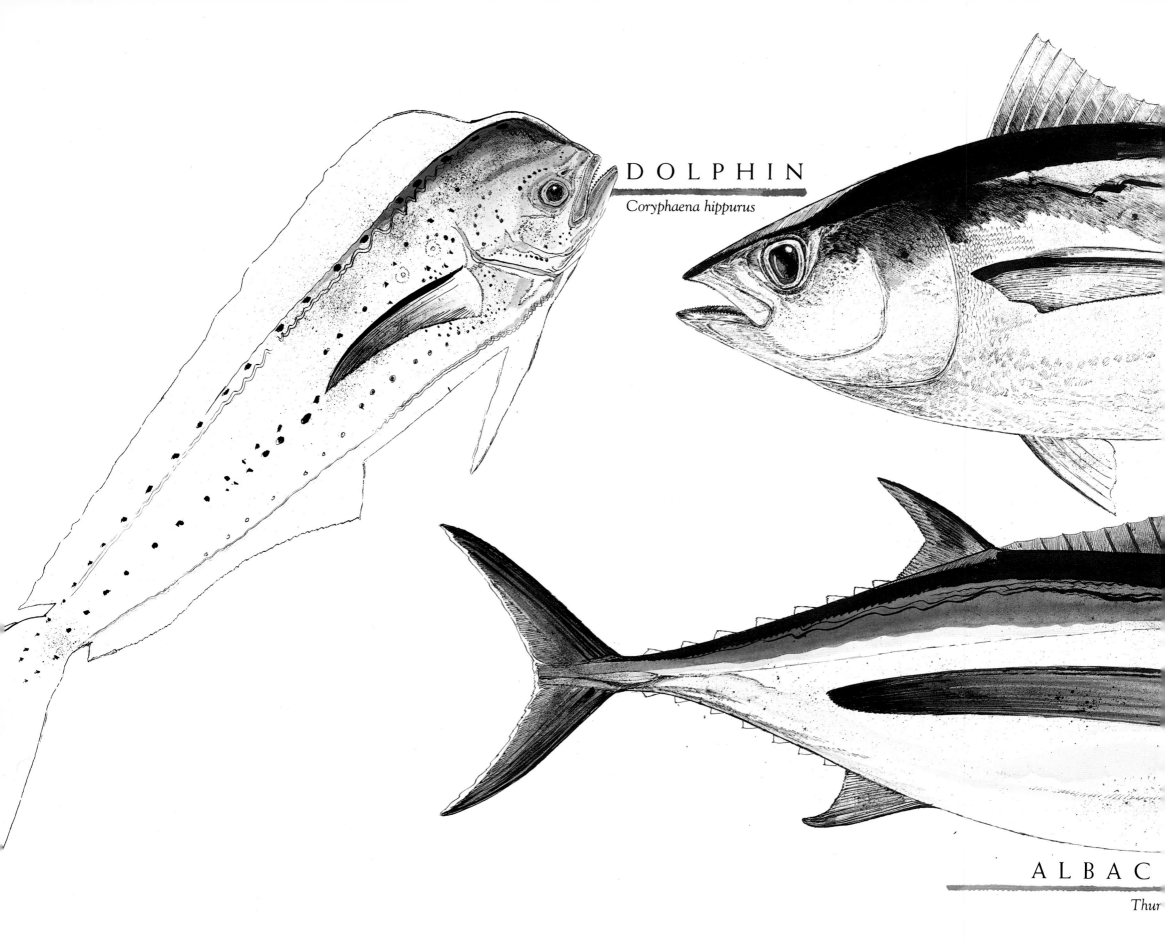

DOLPHIN
Coryphaena hippurus

ALBAC

Thur

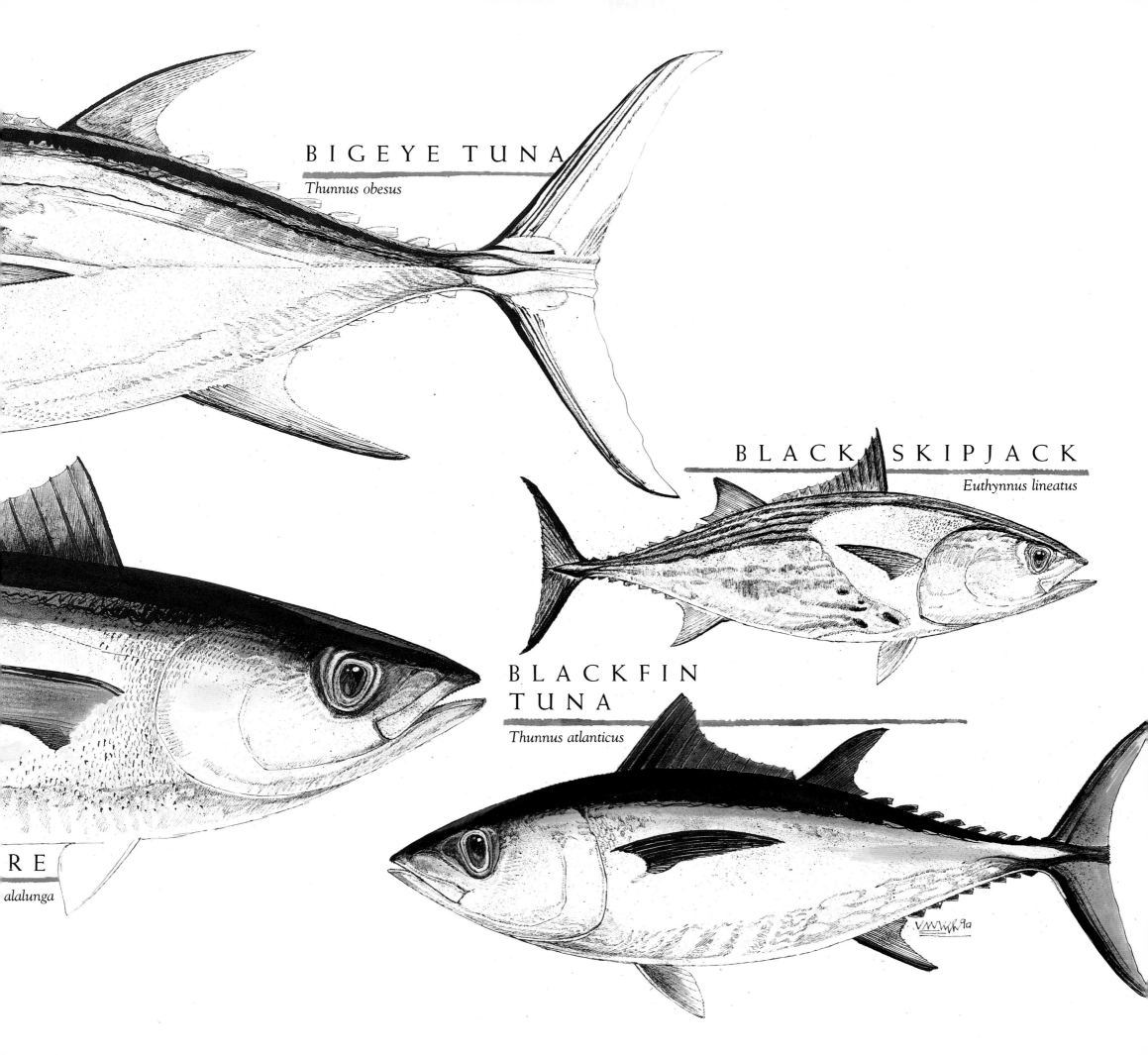

BIGEYE TUNA

Thunnus obesus

BLACK SKIPJACK

Euthynnus lineatus

BLACKFIN TUNA

Thunnus atlanticus

RE

alalunga

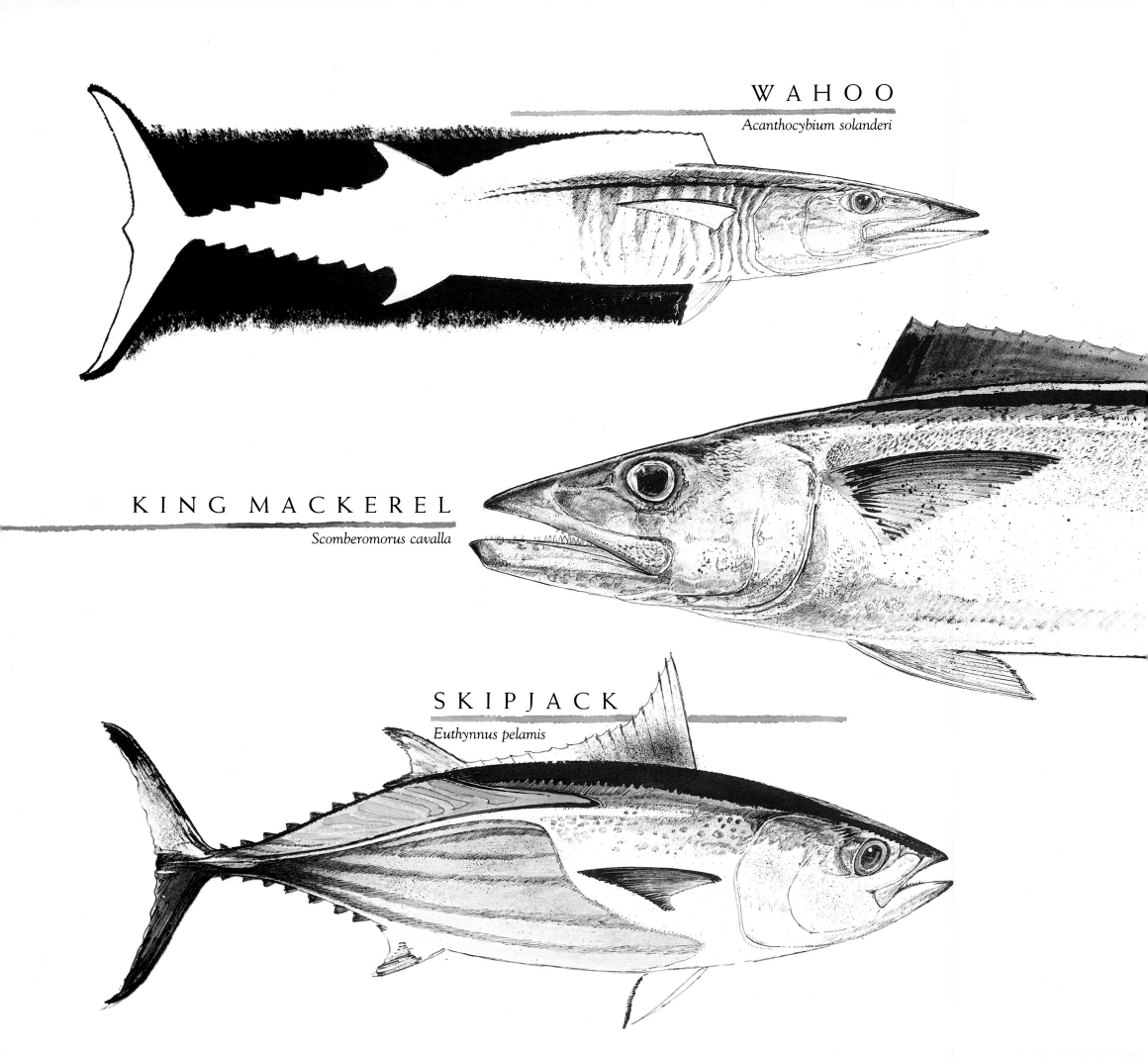

WAHOO
Acanthocybium solanderi

KING MACKEREL
Scomberomorus cavalla

SKIPJACK
Euthynnus pelamis

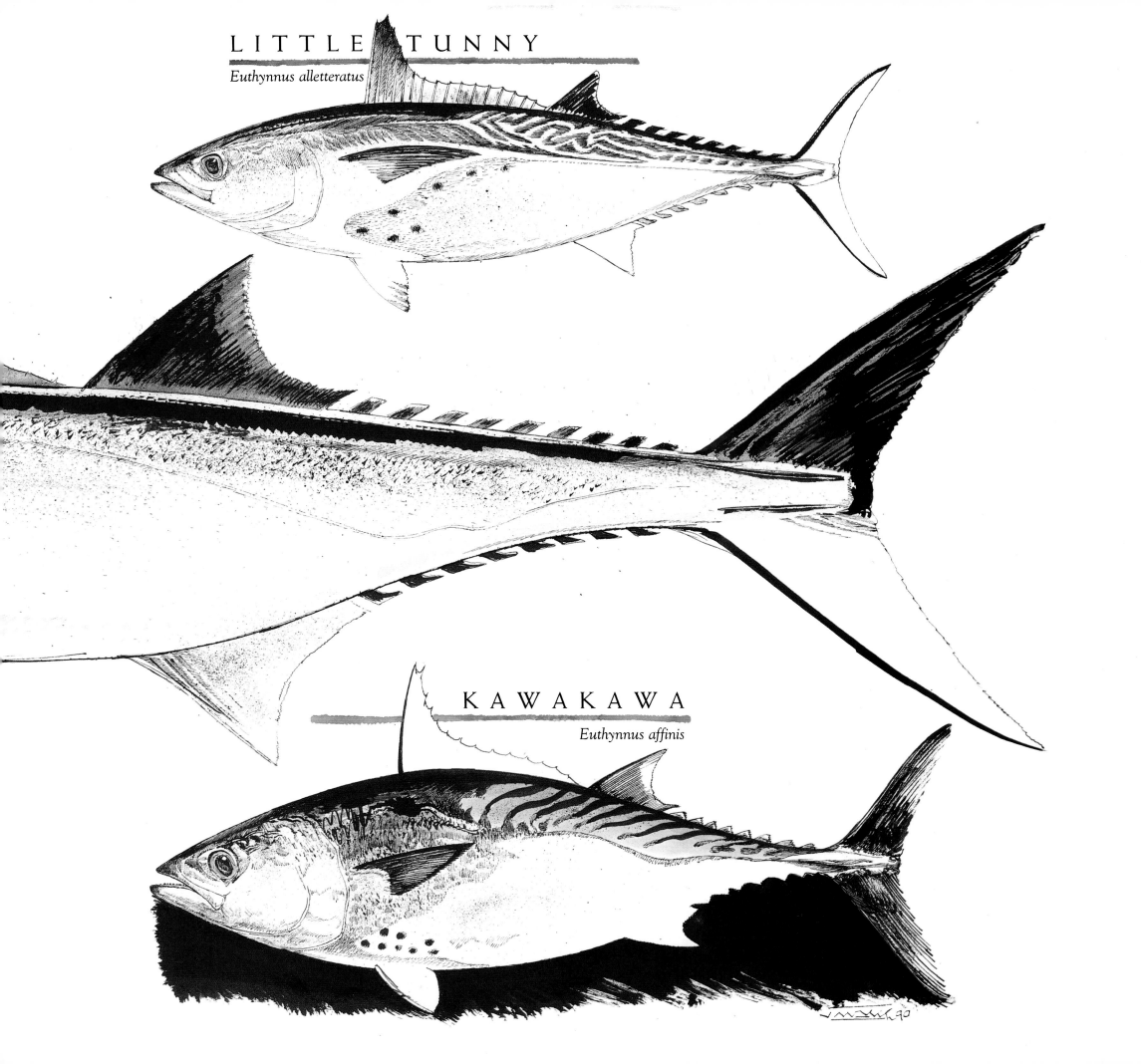

LITTLE TUNNY

Euthynnus alletteratus

KAWAKAWA

Euthynnus affinis

The main rule for planning an offshore big game fishing trip is: Go where the fish are. The international tournament anglers send their boats ahead of them, fly in, fish, play, and get ready for the next hot-spot season. Others with their own boats take sojourns that last weeks or months following the migratory routes of their prey, stopping to fish and explore the territory. By far the majority of anglers who want to catch marlin, swordfish, tuna, and other offshore game fish must compete with other fishermen who are trying to book the same weeks at the same resorts.

Only after considerable experience will an angler learn the subtleties of the sport, including how to get around, and no amount of reading in this book or anywhere else will substitute for that firsthand knowledge converted to instinct. Remember, despite the deluxe quarters in many resorts, the fine restaurants, comfortable yachtlike deep sea boats, and the high-tech electronics and fishing gear, you are still a predator.

One of the best things a novice big game angler can do is read the magazines. Like every passion, offshore fishing has thriving monthly and bimonthly publications whose main business is to sell advertising, but to do so they must hold the reader's interest long enough to keep the pages turning. The advertisements themselves, in many cases, are just about as interesting and informative as the features and news.

A would-be offshore angler should try to become an informed sportsman, as well as find and catch fish. Perhaps most important, though, a new angler should develop a responsible attitude toward the prey. Nothing is more dangerous to the marine environment, and therefore the earth, than humans who interact with complicated systems without a sense of responsibility for that interaction.

Making your prey an object outside your own ecosystem is a terrible mistake, and the chickens will come home to roost on that one

WHERE & WHEN

Planning a Big Game Trip

most certainly. The magazines and literature of big game angling are educational tools to discourage the notion that you can just plunk down a couple of thousand bucks, catch a big fish, and go home. It doesn't work that way, and if you think it does, take up billiards or some nonhunting pastime. (The bibliography contains a list of magazines and other relevant publications.)

The average temperature of the ocean is the main determinant for describing the areas in which marlin, tuna, and other big game fish are likely to be found at different times of the year. Most generally, they migrate seasonally between 30 degrees north and 30 degrees south, the zone in which the water temperature is most often between 60 and 85°F. In midsummer in the Northern Hemisphere, for example, the fish are farthest north, and vice versa in the Southern Hemisphere.

The main geographical exception to this rule occurs when a major current like the Gulf Stream transports warm water into cooler latitudes, as a river would. Therefore, you'll find giant tuna off Nova Scotia in the summer, carried in the warmth of the stream.

All that said, here is a list of the various North American fishing regions and the best times to be at each for your dream fish.

CALIFORNIA

The big game ports of the Southern California coast feature not only day charters but long-range trips of a week or more into the warmer, more prolific waters off Mexico. Charters operate out of Santa Barbara, Oxnard, San Pedro (Los Angeles), Avalon on Santa Catalina Island, Newport Beach, and San Diego.

Swordfish run from May to November; striped marlin, from August to November; tuna, from May to October; and mako, from May to October.

HAWAII

Kona on the Big Island of Hawaii is the place, but fishing charters out of Honolulu, Oahu; Lahaina, Maui; and Kauai also produce marlin, a few swordfish, and tuna.

Blue marlin are best from March to October; the bigger fish come early, late, or in the off-season when the smaller males have migrated elsewhere leaving the giant females with no feeding competition. Striped marlin are found year-round; black marlin, shortbill spearfish, and swordfish are caught occasionally, especially on long-range trips. Tuna can be found year-round.

BAHAMAS/SOUTH ATLANTIC

Bimini is regarded as the spiritual center for billfishing off the Bahamas, and the lore is well supported by results during the right times of the year. Other great Bahamian ports are the very private Walker's Cay, Chub Cay, Treasure Cay, and San Salvador.

Blue marlin are best from April through August, with a peak in June and July; fish are taken year-round in smaller numbers around the islands. White marlin take over for the blues in the winter, with good fishing from November to March or April and occasionally year-round. Sailfish are a summer and fall show, from May to October.

Florida, Georgia, and North and South Carolina—Fish the Gulf Stream as it warms with the seasons and moves closer to the mainland in summer. Blue marlin begin off Florida in

Lee Wulff, angler and writer, fast to a sailfish, using light tackle and a stand-up rig.

May and work north to a midsummer peak off Cape Hatteras, North Carolina; fishing tapers off by August off Florida, and by October off the Carolinas. White marlin are carried north by the Gulf Stream and its eddies as the year warms; generally, they're a May to October show. Off Florida, sailfish are best in winter and spring from December to March; they're farther north during the summer.

GULF OF MEXICO

Alabama, Florida, Louisiana, and Texas—Offshore big game fishing is pretty skinny in the Gulf proper off the U.S. coast, with mostly local boats that do a lot of other kinds of fishing. It isn't a pure big fish charter scene, except along the middle to southern Florida Gulf Coast. Blue marlin peak in the summer, tapering in from April and tailing out in October or so. White marlin and the rare spearfish can be found in the summer. Sailfish make the strongest showing in May and June.

NORTH ATLANTIC

The big fish ride the Gulf Stream north in the summer and that's about all you need to know, generally. There is some sport chartering specifically for big game fish off Virginia, Delaware, Maryland, and New Jersey; more can be found off Long Island, New York, with the legendary Montauk Point area featuring lots of local big fish addicts but not too many guarantees. The human population has destroyed so much marine habitat that a lot of the once-terrific fishing is just a memory.

The big action off the northeast coast is in the upwelling zones of the continental shelf called the Canyons, where the churning eddies of the stream stir up feed, and along the eddies that set up in the summer off Rhode Island and Massachusetts. The fish are deep, and fishermen throw lots of hardware, lights, and time at them, with a lot of night fishing. Tuna, white marlin, and swordfish show in the summer, with the occasional blue marlin. Farther north, tougher fishing awaits off Nova Scotia in late summer and early fall, with the big feature being giant bluefin tuna.

MEXICAN PACIFIC

The ports of Baja and mainland Pacific Mexico are the best bargain for novices who don't really want to get too involved but want to go fishing. There are also many devotees to the region, many private fishermen, and plenty of fish. Cabo San Lucas and the more remote resorts like Rancho Buena Vista on Baja offer spalike living at a fairly reasonable price within six or eight air-hours of most U.S. cities. There is jet service to most ports, with a taxi or shuttle run following to some. The more workaday operations on mainland Mexico across the Sea of Cortez in Guaymas, Mazatlán, Acapulco, and on down are often very productive, but they don't have the charm of the fishing-only resorts. Mexico is a good place to go if you want to fish and do other things.

Blue and black marlin are best from June through October off Baja, starting a month earlier off mainland ports; some fish are taken year-round. Striped marlin start in February and peak in early summer off Baja and in midsummer off the mainland. Sailfish are found year-round, but they're better from May to November off Baja and central mainland ports; good winter sailfish show farther south off Acapulco from November to April.

CARIBBEAN

Just about a paradise as far as variety and easy living go, the many Caribbean ports have much to recommend them to resort fishermen, as well as to roaming anglers with their own outfits, such as refined tourism sensibilities, lots of fish at the right times of year, and fairly easy access via the jet airliner and commuter plane network. With lots of warm water, there's good fishing somewhere all the time as the fish move around and feed in predictable current–temperature patterns.

Belize — Blue marlin and sailfish come from February to April, with a second season in the fall from September to November.

Ted Juracsik, who makes a line of fly reels for big game fishing.

Cayman Islands — Blue marlin are found year-round, peaking in midsummer.

Cozumel (Mexico) — White marlin, sailfish, and occasional blue marlin show from February through July, and peak from March to June.

Cuba — Just starting to open up again to American fishermen, Cuban waters offer blue and white marlin and sailfish in spring and summer.

Dominican Republic — White marlin can be found year-round, but they're best from April through June; some blue marlin can be found at the same time.

Grenada — A great midwinter spot, Grenada's waters harbor blue and white marlin and sailfish from December to May.

Jamaica — Blue and white marlin are best from September to March. Sailfish come from February to June.

Puerto Rico — Blue and white marlin and sailfish are found year-round; the best fishing is from May to September.

Trinidad — Blue and white marlin and sailfish come from November to April, peaking in December.

Virgin Islands — Blue marlin are found from June to September, with the best fishing in August.

OTHER CONSIDERATIONS

In many ports it is possible to simply walk up to a charter outfit and book a trip for that day or the next. In others, bookings are required months in advance and handled either directly or via an agent or clearinghouse in the United States. The best way to become familiar with the charter-resort scene is to buy *Marlin Magazine, Saltwater Sportsman, Sport Fishing,* or *Tournament Digest* and take a trip through the 800 numbers in their advertisements for resorts and charters. A few hours' requesting brochures and getting a feel for the charter owners will do you a world of good. Word of mouth is extremely valuable and reliable in the business of booking a good charter. Ask your fishing friends, and after you've enjoyed a successful trip, get recommendations from that charter owner for other locales.

You can have trouble booking charters or even moorage during peak fishing time in many resorts, so working the "fringe seasons" can be important. The month on either side of prime time can often produce good or even great fishing, depending on the weather and oceanographic conditions. During the El Niño warm trend off California in the early 1980s, for instance, migratory routes extended much farther north than usual and seasons were very different from average. Booking in the fringe seasons can let you down for all the same reasons, but it's worth the look.

When you charter out of one of the major resorts, all gear and usually bait are provided.

Mike Labarbra pulls a sailfish from the Pacific off Golfito, Costa Rica, with a little help from his friends.

with the boat. Many anglers, especially when chartering out of the more remote or undeveloped ports, prefer to bring their own rods, reels, and line to ensure their quality. If you want to use light tackle, bring your own, since charters almost always provide heavy gear in the 80- or 130-pound class unless they specify other gear in their advertisements or when you're booking the trip. The fee for the boat does not include a tip for the crew, which is customary, nor does it include food or beverages.

Other travel considerations such as passports, immunizations, and other international requirements should be handled as you would for any other journey. If you are running your own boat, the details are myriad and you must become familiar with customs and transit regulations for the foreign ports you will visit.

Buddy Davis boat, Merritt boatyard.

BIBLIOGRAPHY

BOOKS

Barrett, Pete. *New Jersey Salt Water Fishing Guide*, 2nd rev. ed. The Fisherman Library. Point Pleasant, N.J.: Ocean Sport Fish, 1985.

Bauer, Erwin A. *Salt Water Fisherman's Bible*, rev. ed. New York: Doubleday, 1983.

Caras, Roger. *Death as a Way of Life*. New York: Little, Brown, 1970.

Danforth, J. T. *Danforth's Guide to Saltwater Fishing*. Hamden, Conn.: Simjac Press, 1986.

Davis, Charlie. *Hook Up*. Self-published, 1977.

Farrington, S. Kip. *Fishing with Hemingway & Glassell*. South Hampton, N.Y.: Yankee Peddler Book Co., n.d.

Hemingway, Ernest. *The Old Man and the Sea*. New York: Scribner's, 1952.

———. *Islands in the Stream*. New York: Scribner's, 1970.

International Game Fish Association. *World Record Game Fishes 1988*. Fort Lauderdale, Fla.: International Game Fish Association, 1989.

Joseph, James, Witold Klawe, and Pat Murphy. *Tuna and Billfish: Fish Without a Country*. La Jolla, Calif.: Inter-American Tropical Tuna Commission, 1980.

Lopez, Barry. *Arctic Dreams*. New York: Scribner's, 1986.

McClane, A. J., ed. *McClane's New Standard Fishing Encyclopedia*. New York: Holt, Rinehart & Winston, 1965.

McGuane, Thomas. *Ninety-Two in the Shade*. New York: Farrar, Straus & Giroux, 1972.

MacLeish, William H. *The Gulf Stream, Encounters with the Blue God*. Boston: Houghton Mifflin, 1989.

Major, Harlan. *Salt Water Fishing Tackle*. New York: Funk & Wagnall, 1948.

Migdalski, Edward C. *Salt Water Game Fishes Atlantic & Pacific*. New York: Ronald Press Co., 1958.

Modern Sea Angler, 6th ed. Philadelphia, Penn.: Trans-Atl-Phila, 1979.

Prichard, Michael, ed. *Sea Angling*. Know the Game Series. Boston, Mass.: Charles River Books, 1976.

Reiger, George. *Profiles in Saltwater Angling*. Englewood Cliffs, N.J.: Prentice-Hall, 1973.

Reiger, George, ed. *The Undiscovered Zane Grey Fishing Stories*. Piscataway, N.J.: Winchester Press, 1983.

Reiger, John F. *American Sportsmen and the Origins of Conservation*, rev. ed. Tulsa: University of Oklahoma, 1986.

Spoczynska, Joy O. I. *An Age of Fishes: The Development of the Most Successful Vertebrate*. New York: Scribner's, 1976.

Steinbeck, John, and Ed Ricketts. *The Log from the Sea of Cortez*. New York: Viking Penguin, 1941.

Thompson, Peter. *The Game Fishes of New England and Southeastern Canada*. Camden, Me.: Down East, 1980.

Woolner, Frank. *Modern Saltwater Sport Fishing*. New York: Crown, 1972.

PERIODICALS

Marlin Magazine, Box 12902, Pensacola, Florida 32576.

National Fisherman, 4055 21st Avenue W., Seattle, Washington 98199.

Oceans Magazine, 2001 W. Main, Stamford, Connecticut 06902.

Oceanus, Woods Hole Oceanographic Institute, Woods Hole, Massachusetts 02543.

Saltwater Sportsman, 280 Summer Street, Boston, Massachusetts 02210.

Sport Fishing Magazine, 5885 SW 2nd Street, Miami, Florida 33144.

Tournament Digest, 2855 NW 75th Avenue, Miami, Florida 33122.

Deep Sea Fishing: The Lure of Big Fish was
produced in association with the publisher by
McQuiston & Partners in Del Mar, California:
art direction, Don McQuiston; design, Joyce Sweet;
editorial supervision, Tom Chapman;
mechanical production, Joyce Sweet and
Kristi Paulson Mendola; copyediting, Robin Witkin;
illustrations, Jack Unruh; composition, TypeLink;
text type, Goudy Old Style;
text paper, 157-gsm Glossy Coated; printed in
Japan by Dai Nippon Printing Co., Ltd.